MCDP 1-1

Strategy

U.S. Marine Corps

PCN 142 000007 00

DEPARTMENT OF THE NAVY
Headquarters United States Marine Corps
Washington, D.C. 20380-1775

12 November 1997

FOREWORD

This publication is designed to give Marine leaders a solid, common understanding of the fundamental nature of military strategy that is inherent in each military action. Its intent is to give the reader the basic knowledge required to think "strategically," that is, to be able to examine the particulars of any specific situation and understand the political and military factors behind the use of military force.

Marine Corps Doctrinal Publication (MCDP) 1-1 provides the foundation for thinking strategically. This foundation will enable Marines to better understand their roles in a particular situation and to consider the implications of their actions on the military strategy being employed and the political objectives that strategy is intended to achieve.

Just as it is important to appreciate what this publication is designed to do, it is equally important to understand what this publication does not seek to do. It does not attempt to provide a solution to current strategic problems, nor is it concerned with details of current American strategy. MCDP 1-1 does not assume that war and military strategy are exclusively a matter of international or interstate behavior, and the concepts discussed in it are not limited to any particular *kind* of warfare or level of conflict. Nor does *Strategy* prescribe any particular strategy, any particular process for the making of strategy, or any specific techniques and procedures for handling military forces. It is meant to educate the mind of future commanders or, more accurately, to guide them in their self-education, not to accompany them to the battlefield.

Chapter 1 explores the complex nature of the strategic environment, including the relationship between war and politics and the key factors at work in any strategic situation. Chapter 2 discusses the essential elements of any strategy, the relationship of ends and means, and the interaction among political objectives, national strategy, and military strategy. Chapter 3 looks at a variety of strategies as they might be developed in different strategic situations. Chapter 4 synthesizes the concepts presented in the first three chapters by focusing on how strategy is made, who makes it, what moral criteria guide strategic decisions, and what pitfalls may occur in the making of strategy.

This publication is primarily for field grade officers. However, Marines at all levels require a broad perspective and an understanding of how the effects of their actions can influence the attainment of our national objectives. Furthermore, Marines of any rank or specialty can easily find themselves working for senior leaders with strategic responsibilities. Those leaders need subordinates who understand the strategic environment and can provide intelligent and insightful ad- vice on the strategic situation. Therefore, as a foundation for strategic thought, this publication should be read and under- stood by Marines at all levels of command both in the operating forces and the supporting establishment.

C. C. KRULAK
General, U.S. Marine Corps
Commandant of the Marine Corps

DISTRIBUTION: 142 000007 00

Unless otherwise specified, masculine nouns and pronouns used in this manual refer to both men and women.

Strategy

Introduction. The Study of Strategy

Chapter 1.   The Strategic Environment

The Nature of Politics and War—Further Defining War—
The Nature of War-Making Political Entities—Strategic
Constants and Norms–*The Physical Environment–*
National Character–War and the State–The Balance of
Power Mechanism—The Trinity

Chapter 2.   Strategy: Ends and Means

National Strategy—Ends in National Strategy–*Survival*
and Victory–Political Objectives—Means in National
Strategy—Adapting Ends to Means, and Vice Versa—
Ends in Military Strategy–*Relationship Between Political*
and Military Objectives–Distinguishing Between Erosion
and Annihilation Strategies

Introduction

The Study of Strategy

"The nation that draws too great a distinction between its scholars and its warriors will have its thinking done by cowards and its fighting done by fools."[1]

—Unknown

M arine Corps Doctrinal Publication (MCDP) 1, *War-fighting*, stresses that war is fundamentally political in character and that war must serve policy. What matters ultimately in war is strategic success: attainment of our political aims and the protection of our national interests. History shows that national leaders, both political and military, who fail to understand this relationship sow the seeds for ultimate failure—even when their armed forces achieve initial battlefield success. Battlefield brilliance seldom rescues a bad strategy.

The United States Marine Corps is a key instrument in the execution of American national strategy. Marine expeditionary forces possess extraordinary strategic reach. As an expeditionary force-in-readiness, the Marine Corps has been consistently called upon to implement key elements of our national security strategy and its supporting national military strategy. While the Marine Corps is not a strategy-making organization in the sense of designing a national military strategy or even drafting strategies to fight particular wars, the effective execution of strategy requires an understanding of both its intent and its context. In order to carry out our responsibilities to the Nation, Marines must possess the strategic skills and understanding necessary to participate effectively in the strategic environment of the 21st century

There are three important reasons to develop a fundamental understanding of strategy:

- Marines will find themselves working for senior leaders who participate directly in the development of strategy. Such leaders need subordinates who understand their requirements and the environment they work in.

- An understanding of how strategy is made allows Marines to see the larger picture. It enables them to better grasp the intent that underlies the military actions in which they participate and the constraints placed upon the use of military force during these actions. It also helps Marine leaders provide useful answers to questions posed by their subordinates concerning the purpose and objectives behind our involvement in a particular operation.

- By the very nature of their profession, all Marines are engaged in the execution of strategy. Every military action has potential strategic implications. Modern media coverage has intensified both the awareness of and sensitivity towards any military action. Marines must understand that the "distance" between local or tactical actions and the effects of these actions at the strategic or political level may be very short. Sometimes a seemingly unimportant action by any participant—a general, a platoon leader, or even one single Marine—can have a powerful political impact.

MCDP 1-1 focuses on military strategy in its most fundamental sense, exploring the question "How do military means relate to political ends?" It provides a conceptual basis to help us to understand both our own and our enemies' political and military objectives, the relationships among them, and the nature of any particular situation in which military means might be used. It explores how political entities integrate military means with the other elements of their power in order to attain their political ends. A common conceptual understanding of these matters helps *Marines develop the adaptability that our warfighting philosophy demands.*

Chapter 1

The Strategic Environment

"The roots of victory and defeat often have to be sought far from the battlefield, in political, social, and economic factors which explain why armies are constituted as they are, and why their leaders conduct them in the way they do."[1]

—Michael Howard

"That the factors are infinitely varied and difficult to determine is true, but that . . . is just what emphasises the necessity of reaching such firm standpoints as are attainable. The vaguer the problem to be solved, the more resolute must we be in seeking points of departure from which we can begin to lay a course."[2]

—Julian Corbett

A t its most basic, strategy is a matter of figuring out what we need to achieve, determining the best way to use the resources at our disposal to achieve it, and then executing the plan. Unfortunately, in the real world, all of these things are not easily done. Our strategic goals are complex and sometimes contradictory and may change in the middle of a military endeavor. The resources at our disposal are not always obvious, can change during the course of a struggle, and usually need to be adapted to suit our needs. Our adversary often refuses to fit our preconceptions of him or to stand still while we erect the apparatus for his destruction.

THE NATURE OF POLITICS AND WAR

Before we can usefully discuss the making and carrying out of military strategy, we must understand the fundamental character of politics and the violent expression of politics called war. Let us start by analyzing Clausewitz's description of war as both an instrument of policy and of politics with the addition of other means.[3]

War is a social phenomenon. Its logic is not the logic of art, nor of science or engineering, but rather the logic of social transactions. Human beings interact with each other in ways that are fundamentally different from the way the scientist interacts with chemicals, the architect or engineer with beams and girders, or the artist with paints. The interaction that concerns us when we speak of war is political interaction. The "other means" in Clausewitz's definition of war is organized violence. The addition of violence to political interaction is the only factor that defines war as a distinct form of political interaction—but that addition has powerful and unique effects.

The two different terms we have used, policy and politics, both concern *power*. While every specific war has its unique causes, war as a phenomenon is fundamentally concerned with the distribution and redistribution of power.[4]

Power is sometimes material in nature: the economic power of money or other resources, for example, or possession of the physical means for coercion (weapons and armed personnel). Power is just as often psychological in nature: legal, religious, or scientific authority; intellectual or social prestige; a charismatic personality's ability to excite or persuade; a reputation, accurate or illusory, for diplomatic or military strength.

Power provides the means to attack and the means to resist attack. Power in itself is neither good nor evil. By its nature, however, power tends to be distributed unevenly in ways that vary greatly from one society to another.

Power manifests itself differently and in different places at different times. In Japan, during the 16th through 19th centuries, real political power was exercised by the shogun, who was formally subordinate to the emperor. Later, senior Japanese military leaders were for a time effectively controlled by

10

groups of fanatical junior officers. King Philip II of Spain, whose power was rooted in a landed aristocracy, was surprised to discover the power that Europe's urban bankers could exercise over his military strategy. American leaders were similarly surprised by the power of the disparate political coalition that forced an end to the Vietnam War. One of the major problems of strategy is to determine where and in what form real power lies and to identify those relatively rare points where military power can be applied effectively.

Politics is the process by which power is *distributed* in any society: a family, an office, a religious order, a tribe, a state, a region, the international community. The process of distributing power may be fairly orderly—through consensus, inheritance, election, or some time-honored tradition—or chaotic—through assassination, revolution, or warfare. Whatever process may be in place at any given time, politics is inherently dynamic, and not only the distribution of power but the process by which it is distributed is under constant pressure for change.

A key characteristic of politics is that it is interactive—a cooperative or competitive process. It cannot be characterized as a rational process because actual outcomes are seldom what was consciously intended by any one of the participants. Political events and their outcomes are the product of conflicting, contradictory, sometimes compromising, but often adversarial forces. That description clearly applies to war.

Policy, on the other hand, *can* be characterized as a rational process. The making of policy is a conscious effort by a

distinct political body to use whatever power it possesses to accomplish some purpose—if only the mere continuation or increase of its own power. Policy is a rational subcomponent of
politics, the reasoned purposes and actions of individuals in the
political struggle. War can be a practical means, sometimes the
only means available, for the achievement of rational policy
aims—that is, the aims of one party in the political dispute.
*Hence, to describe war as an "instrument of policy" is en-
tirely correct. It is an act of force to compel our opponent to
do our will.*

Do not, however, confuse rationality with intelligence, rea-
sonableness, or understanding. Policies can be wise or foolish:
they can advance their creators' goals or unwittingly contradict
them. They can be driven by concern for the public good or by
the most craven reasons of self-interest. Rationality also implies no particular *kind* of goal, for goals are a product of emotion and human desire. The goal of policy may be peace and
prosperity, national unity, the achievement of ideological per-
fection, or the extermination of some ethnic minority or
competitor.

Remember too that policy, while it is different from politics,
is produced via a political process. Even the most rational of
policies is often the result of compromises within the political
group. Such compromises may be intended more to maintain
peace or unity within the group than to accomplish any external purpose. They may, in fact, be irrelevant or contrary to any
explicit group goal. Policy is therefore often ambiguous,

unclear, even contradictory, and subject to change or to rigidity when change is needed.

Clausewitz's reference to war as an expression of politics is therefore not a prescription, but a description. War is a part of politics. It does not replace other forms of political intercourse but merely supplements them. It is a violent expression of the tensions and disagreements between political groups, when political conflict reaches a level that sparks organized violence. Thus war—like every other phase of politics—embodies both rational and irrational elements. Its course is the product not of one will, but of the collision of two or more wills.

To say, then, that war is an expression of both politics and policy with the addition of other means is to say two very different things to strategy makers. First, it says that strategy, insofar as it is a conscious and rational process, must strive to achieve the policy goals set by the political leadership. Second, it says that such policy goals are created only within the chaotic and emotional realm of politics.

Therefore, the military professional who says, "Keep politics out of this. Just give us the policy, and we will take care of the strategy," does not understand the fundamentals of

strategy. Strategists must operate within the constraints of policy and politics. The only alternative would be for military strategy to perform the functions of policy and for military

leaders to usurp political power, tasks which are generally un-
suited to both military strategy and military leaders.

FURTHER DEFINING WAR

We acknowledge that war is an expression of politics and policy with the addition of violent means. Still, this description
does not fully explain war.

One frequent error is to describe war as something that takes
place exclusively between nations or states. First, nations and
states are different things. The Kurds are a nation, but they
have no state. The Arabs are a nation with several states. The
Soviet Union was a state whose citizens represented many different nationalities. Second, many—possibly most— wars actually take place within a single state, meaning that at least one
of the participants was not previously a state. Civil wars, in-
surrections, wars of secession, and revolutions all originate
within a single existing state, although they sometimes attract
external intervention. Wars may spill across state borders without being interstate wars, as in Turkey's conflict with the
Kurds. Third, most interstate wars are fought not by individual
states, but by coalitions. Such coalitions often involve nonstate
actors as well as state govern- ments.
Another mistake is to limit our definition of war to sus-
tained, large-scale military operations. Here the defining condi-
tion is one of scale and duration. Under headings such as
"Military Operations Other than War," this approach lumps

14

many forms of political conflict that clearly satisfy Clausewitz's definition of war with other events—such as humanitarian assistance—that do not.

In its broadest sense, war refers to any use of organized force for political purposes, whether that use results in actual violence or not. When we speak of warfare, however, we almost always mean actual violence of some considerable scale that is carried out over some considerable period of time. A single assassination, while certainly a violent political act, does not constitute a war. On the other hand, large-scale, long-term violence alone does not necessarily mean war either. For example, over a 25-year period—1969 through 1994—some 3,000 people were killed in Northern Ireland for an average of 120 deaths per year in a population of 1.5 million.[5] For that same period, there were approximately 291 murders per year committed in Washington, D.C. in an average population of 642,000.[6] The former situation is widely recognized as war, while the latter is not. The difference is a matter of organization. The perpetrators, victims, and targets of the violence in Northern Ireland reflect distinct political groups engaged in a power struggle. The violent death rate in Washington, D.C., roughly five times higher, seems to reflect random violence—a sign of social dysfunction rather than of some purposeful group movement toward any political goal.

From all this, we can say that war is—

• Organized violence.

- Waged by two or more distinguishable groups against each other.

- In pursuit of some political end.

- Sufficiently large in scale and in social impact to attract the attention of political leaders.

- Continued long enough for the interplay between the opponents to have some impact on political events.

THE NATURE OF WAR-MAKING POLITICAL ENTITIES

Military professionals often seek a "scientific" understanding of war. This approach is appealing because the human mind tends to organize its perceptions according to familiar analogies, like the powerful images of traditional Newtonian physics. Such comparisons can be very useful. Our military doctrine abounds with terms like "center of gravity," "mass," and "friction."

The attempt to apply a scientific approach can result in some misleading ideas. For example, some political scientists treat political entities as unitary rational actors, the social equivalents of Newton's solid bodies hurtling through space. Real political units, however, are not unitary. Rather, they are collections of intertwined but fundamentally distinct actors and systems. Their behavior derives from the internal interplay of both rational and irrational forces as well as from the peculiarities of their own histories and of chance. Strategists who accept the unitary rational actor model as a description of adversaries at war will have difficulty understanding either side's motivations or actual behavior. Such strategists ignore their own side's greatest potential vulnerabilities and deny themselves potential levers and targets—the fault lines that exist within any human political construct.

Fortunately, the physical sciences have begun to embrace the class of problems posed by social interactions like politics and war. The appropriate imagery, however, is not that of Newtonian physics. Rather, we need to think in terms of biology and particularly ecology.[7]

To survive over time, the various members of any ecosystem must adapt—not only to the external environment, but to each other. These agents compete or cooperate, consume and are consumed, join and divide, and so on. A system created by such interaction is called a complex adaptive system.

Such systems are inherently dynamic. Although they may sometimes appear stable for lengthy periods, their components constantly adapt or fail. No species evolves alone; rather, each species "co-evolves" with the other species that make up its environment. The mutation or extinction of one species in any ecosystem has a domino or ripple effect throughout the system, threatening damage to some species and creating opportunities for others. Slight changes are sometimes absorbed without unbalancing the system. Other slight changes—an alteration in the external environment or a local mutation—can send the system into convulsions of growth or collapse.

One of the most interesting things about complex systems is that they are inherently unpredictable. It is impossible, for example, to know in advance which slight perturbations in an ecological system will settle out unnoticed and which will spark catastrophic change. This is so not because of any flaw in our understanding of such systems, but because the system's behavior is generated according to rules the system itself develops and is able to alter. In other words, a system's behavior may be constrained by external factors or laws but is not determined by them.

For all of these reasons, systems starting from a similar base come to have unique individual characteristics based on their specific histories.

The reason we use the complex adaptive system as a model is that it provides insight into human political constructs. Humans build all sorts of social structures: families, tribes, clans, social classes, street gangs, armies, religious groups or sects, commercial corporations, political parties, bureaucracies, criminal mafias, states of various kinds, alliances, and empires, to mention just a few. These structures participate in separate but thoroughly intertwined networks we call social, economic, and political systems. Those networks produce markets, elections, and wars.

18

Such networks and structures create their own rules. The unpredictable nature of these complex systems makes it difficult to predict the outcome of specific events. We can normally analyze, describe, and explain economic, military, and political events after they have occurred, but accurately forecasting the course of such interactions is difficult to do with any consistency.

When we say that politics and war are unpredictable, we do not mean that they are composed of absolute chaos, without any semblance of order. *Intelligent, experienced military and political leaders are generally able to foresee the probable near-term results, or at least a range of possible results, of any particular action they may take.* Broad causes, such as a massive superiority in manpower, technology, economic resources, and military skill, will definitely influence the probabilities of certain outcomes.

Conscious actions, however, like evolutionary adaptations, seldom have only their intended effects. Events wholly outside the range of vision of political and military leaders can have an unforeseen impact on the situation. New economic and social ideas, technological innovations with no obvious military applications, changes in climatic conditions, demographic shifts, all can lead to dramatic political and military changes. Enemy actions, friction, imperfect knowledge, low order probabilities, and chance introduce new variables into any evolving situation.

19

The problem for strategists is how to develop a lasting and effective strategy in the face of the turbulent world of policy and politics. Despite the difficulty of understanding the interaction of political entities, they must strive to comprehend the nature of the problem, anticipate possible outcomes, and set a strategic course likely to achieve the desired objective. At the same time, strategists must sense the complex nature of this environment and be prepared for both the unexpected setbacks and the sudden opportunities it is likely to deliver.

STRATEGIC CONSTANTS AND NORMS

In *Some Principles of Maritime Strategy*, originally published in 1911, Sir Julian Corbett wrote—

> The vaguer the problem to be solved, the more resolute must we be in seeking points of departure from which we begin to lay a course, keeping always an eye open for the accidents that will beset us, and being always alive to their deflecting influences . . . . [T]he theoretical study of strategy . . . can at least determine the normal. By careful collation of past events it becomes clear that certain lines of conduct tend normally to produce certain effects.[8]

Despite the complexity of interactions in the political realm, it is possible to discern elements that are present in any strategic situation. These elements are at the core of the strategic environment and are the base from which the strategist develops an understanding of a specific set of circumstances. Because these elements are present in any strategic situation, we refer to them as constants and norms. While the particular aspects of these constants and norms present themselves differently in each strategic situation, an understanding of their fundamental nature provides a point of departure for its analysis.

To help understand the distinction between constants and norms and the fluctuations of a specific policy or conflict, we can use the following analogy. Annual seasonal climates of most regions of the world are predictable. Yet the weather on a given day cannot be predicted far in advance with any confidence. Still, annual vacationers in northern Pennsylvania know that a warm day in January is colder than a cold day in July, and a snow skier does not plan a ski trip for July, nor does a water skier plan on water skiing in January. Extreme variables in temporary weather patterns do not affect the long-term power and influence of global climate patterns.

The Physical Environment
Geography and its related aspects are a constant in any strategic situation. All parties in a conflict must cope with the physical environment. One strategic affairs expert has noted—

Misguided strategists who misinterpret, misapply, or ignore the crushing impact of geography on national security affairs learn their lessons painfully, after squandering national prestige, lives, and treasure.

Strategic masters manipulate the physical environment, exploit its strengths, evade its weaknesses, acknowledge constraints, and contrive always to make nature work for them.[9]

The physical environment encompasses not only the traditional elements of geography such as land forms, terrain, oceans and seas, and climate, but also spatial relationships, natural resources, and lines of communications. Together, these factors exert considerable influence on a particular strategic situation. The political, economic, and social makeup of a nation results in part from its physical environment. We refer to Great Britain, the United States, and Japan as "maritime nations," while Germany, Russia, and China have been traditionally labeled "continental powers." The location and distribution of natural resources may on the one hand be a cause of conflict and, at the same time, be a major determinant of a conflict's outcome. The nature of the interaction between political entities is in large part determined by their geographic relationships. Relations between states that border on one another are normally considerably different from those between states separated by oceans and continents.

In order to understand the nature of a problem, *strategists must understand the role of the physical environment in each situation.* Geography influences the way that all elements of national power are applied. While the effect of geography on a conflict varies with the nature, location, and duration of that conflict, the physical environment always has an impact. Strategists must analyze and understand the local, regional, and sometimes global effects of this environment in order to use the elements of power effectively in a specific strategic situation.[10]

National Character

Each nation, state, or political entity has its own distinct character. This character is derived from a variety of sources: location, language, culture, religion, historical circumstances, and so forth. While national character is always evolving, changes generally occur only over the course of decades and centuries and may be imperceptible to the outside observer. As such, national character can be looked upon as a norm or constant. National character is akin to global climate patterns that change very slowly through history.

Over three centuries, the British national character ran as deep and sure as the Gulf Stream across the North Atlantic. During this time, British national reaction to aggression from France, Germany, or, more recently, Argentina, was marked by many constants. Throw in a resolute and inspirational leader (the elder William Pitt, Winston Churchill, or Margaret Thatcher), add a villainous opponent bent on European domination (Napoleon, the Kaiser, or Hitler), and the British response to aggression was both consistent and predictable.

This is not to say that the British reacted the same way in each situation. The mood and inclination of the British public have been influenced by various swirls and eddies during periods and moments when issues were confused, threats ambiguous, and hopes for peace strong. For example, the British first attempted to avoid war with Germany by acceding to Hitler's demands at the now infamous Munich Conference of 1938. Then when Germany invaded Poland a year later, natural inclinations and hopes for peace vanished into a steeled determination to wage war.

Consider too the Russian response to invasions from the West. The Russians have never deliberately adopted a strategy of retreating hundreds of miles into their interior without first trying to stop an invader near their borders. The point is that they have demonstrated an *ability* to retreat deeply into their own country if they must do so in order to survive and ultimately prevail. This demonstrated ability was a matter of historical record to be considered by Charles XII of Sweden in 1708, Napoleon in 1812, Kaiser Wilhelm III in 1914, and Hitler in 1941. It is no coincidence that of these invaders, the only one to succeed (Germany in World War I) was the one that adopted a strategy containing a viable political component, in this case the support of internal revolution, used in conjunction with the military component. The Germans in World War I considered knowable Russian physical and moral characteristics and devised an effective political-military strategy accordingly. Napoleon and Hitler had access to similar knowledge but largely ignored the Russian character in relying on a purely military strategy.

Judging the national character of an adversary (or an ally) goes well beyond traditional orders of battle and related calculations regarding military and economic power. It requires consideration of national history, culture, religion, society, politics—everything that contributes to the makeup and functioning of a nation. The strategist must compile a complete dossier on a nation similar to that commonly prepared on enemy commanders. In the popular movie *Patton*, an impatient Field Marshal Rommel interrupts his aide: "Enough! Tell me about the man" (referring to General Patton). Rommel wanted to know about Patton's personality: Was he a gambler? Would he attack sooner rather than later? What was his style of warfare and leadership? What did his troops think of him? Rommel wanted a psychological profile of the opposing commander to help him understand his adversary. At the strategic level, success in war is facilitated by having a similar comprehensive psychological profile of each nation or political group involved in the conflict, to include enemies, allies, potential enemies or allies, and even one's own nation.

It is of critical importance that sweeping dogmatic assertions do not govern the analysis of national characters. Such assertions often spring from ethnocentristic attitudes and a failure to examine the true nature of a political presence. Rather, what is required is rational, objective, and informed thought about the makeup of a national character and its possible effects on a nation's action or reaction to an event.

War and the State

The state has been effective in all forms of politics, including war. It has been so effective, in fact, that virtually all of the world's land surface and its people are now recognized as belonging to some more or less effective territorial state. While entities other than the state make war, a state will almost always become involved either in self-defense or in assertion of its monopoly on the legitimate use of violence. Thus, we must look upon the state as one of the strategic norms or constants when we are confronted with a specific strategic problem.

While it has been said that "war made the state, and the state made war,"[11] the state has over time held in remarkable check the human tendency toward violence. Averaged over the first 90 years of the 20th century, even Germany's annual rate of war deaths is lower than that of many typical primitive societies.[12] Although warfare between states has continued, successful states have been able to control the costly endemic local warfare typical of nonstate societies.

States are normally replaced by other states. If a state fails to control the use of violence, it will likely be destroyed or taken over by some new group willing and able to take on this fundamental function of the state. This new leadership may be another state or possibly a supranational alliance like the North Atlantic Treaty Organization (NATO) or the United Nations. It could also be a revolutionary government evolving out of what was formerly a nonstate political presence.

26

This is not to say that states or the interrelated system of states does not change or that strategists can always rely on stability in the international arena. From 1950 to 1980 in Africa, 47 new states won their independence. In late 1988, after 73 years of colonial rule, Africa's last colony, Namibia, gained its independence.[13] The United States, which sees itself as a young state, in fact has the oldest constitutional system on earth. Many people alive today were born when most of Europe was ruled by kings or emperors. Powerful states and ideologies, commanding formidable military machines, have entered and left the world stage while those people grew up. The Soviet Union, one of the most powerful nations in human history, covering a sixth of the world's surface and encompassing hundreds of millions of human beings, lasted less than a human lifetime.

However, on balance, we can look upon the state as remarkably tough and enduring. While political movements and individual states and governments that wage wars evolve and change, we must address any particular conflict or strategic problem in the context of the state system. Strategists must take into account the actions and reactions not only of their adversary, but also the actions and reactions of other states and nations. At the same time, we should remember that there is nothing permanent about any particular political entity. This lack of permanence is important because it reminds us that every enemy, no matter how seamless and monolithic it may appear, has political fault lines that can be exploited.

The Balance of Power Mechanism

We have already noted that politics and policy are concerned with the distribution of power and that conflict often arises out of attempts to change the distribution of power. One of the ways political entities achieve stability in the distribution of power and avoid a continuous state of conflict is by seeking to maintain a "balance of power." The balance of power is a mechanism intended to maintain the status quo in the distribu-tion of power.[14] It describes a system in which alliances shift in order to ensure that no one entity or group of entities becomes dominant. The balance of power is "at once the dominant myth and the fundamental law of interstate re- lations."[15]

The term "balance of power" is usually used in reference to states, but it is applicable to any system involving more than one political power center. The balance of power can be global, as it was during the Cold War, regional/local, as it was among Iran, Iraq, Saudi Arabia, and the other Persian Gulf states, or internal to one state or territory, as it was among the various clans in Somalia.

Balance of power considerations are usually at work in any strategic situation. Thus, we can consider the balance of power as a strategic norm or constant. Balance of power systems have appeared frequently in world history. Normally, such a system is created when several entities vie for supremacy or at least in-dependence, yet none individually has the power to achieve it alone.

A balance of power system breaks down for two reasons. The first is when one or more of the participants in the system rebel against it. Their goal is to eliminate all competitors and achieve dominance. In modern Europe, this goal has been at-tempted by a number of states and their leaders such as Ger-many under Hitler and France under Napolcon. The rebels have never fully succeeded, largely because they have to take on multiple enemies. Ambitious powers must always be wary of what Clausewitz called the culminating point of victory.[16] This is the point at which one competitor's success prompts its allies and other groups to withdraw their support or even throw their weight against it.

The second threat to the balance of power system is the power vacuum that occurs when there is no authority capable of maintaining order in some geographic area. Power vacuums are disruptive to the balance of power in two distinct ways. First, the disorder in the vacuum tends to spread as violent ele-ments launch raids into surrounding areas or commit other pro-vocative acts. The disintegration of the Soviet Union in the early 1990s has provided many examples of this sort. Another example is the disintegration of Yugoslavia that resulted in NATO intervention in Bosnia. Second, a power vacuum may attract annexation by an external power. If this act threatens to add substantially to the annexing entity's power, other states will become concerned and may interfere. Many Russians saw NATO's intervention in Bosnia in this light. NATO's agreement to Russian participation in that mission was an attempt to mitigate such concerns.

Some have argued that the balance of power is no longer a useful concept in the post-Cold War world dominated by a single military superpower. However, it is clear that on a regional and local level the concept of balance of power remains a useful basis for strategic analysis. The balancing mechanism remains a useful strategic tool and is applicable to all levels.

Strategists must be aware of the dynamics of various balance of power systems involved in a strategic problem. Like the "invisible hand" of market economics, the balance of power mechanism is always at work, regardless of whether the system's participants believe that it is a good thing. It influences our actions as well as those of our adversaries, allies, and neutral powers.

Consider the case of the Gulf War. One of the motives for participation in the conflict by the U.S. and other Coalition forces was concern over the prospect of a region dominated by Iraq. Conversely, one of the postwar concerns was to avoid the creation of a power vacuum that could lead to increased instability in the region or greater influence by Iran. Finally, the dynamics of relations within the Coalition also involved reconciling sometimes differing views on balance of power issues. In any coalition, some participants may be only temporary allies with long-term goals that may diverge widely from one another. Thus, balance of power considerations were at work from start to finish during this conflict.

THE TRINITY

This chapter has described the nature of the strategic environment. This environment is defined by the nature of politics and the interactions of political entities that participate in the political process. The strategic environment is complex and subject to the interplay of dynamic and often contradictory factors. Some elements of politics and policy are rational, that is, the product of conscious thought and intent. Other aspects are governed by forces that defy rational explanation. We can discern certain factors that are at work in any strategic situation—the constants and norms—and use them as a framework to help understand what is occurring. At the same time, we realize that each strategic situation is unique and that in order to grasp its true nature, we must comprehend how the character and motivations of each of the antagonists will interact in these specific circumstances.

Summarizing the environment within which war and strategy are made, Clausewitz described it as being dominated by a "remarkable trinity" that is—

composed of primordial violence, hatred, and enmity, which are to be regarded as a blind natural force; of the play of chance and probability within which the creative spirit is free to roam; and of [war's] element of subordination, as an instrument of policy, which makes it subject to reason alone.

The first of these three aspects mainly concerns the people; the second the commander and his army; the third the government.

These three tendencies are like three different codes of law, deep-rooted in their subject and yet variable in their relationship to one another. A theory that ignores any one of them or seeks to fix an arbitrary relationship between them would conflict with reality to such an extent that for this reason alone it would be totally useless.

Our task therefore is to develop a theory that maintains a balance between these three tendencies, like an object suspended between three magnets.[17]

Clausewitz concluded that the strategic environment is shaped by the disparate forces of emotion, chance, and rational thought. At any given moment, one of these forces may dominate, but the other two are always at work. The actual course of events is determined by the dynamic interplay among them. The effective strategist must master the meaning and the peculiarities of this environment.[18]

Chapter 2

Strategy: Ends and Means

"You [military professionals] must know something about strategy and tactics and logistics, but also economics and politics and diplomacy and history. You must know everything you can about military power, and you must also understand the limits of military power.

You must understand that few of the problems of our time have . . . been solved by military power alone."[1]

—John F. Kennedy

S trategy, broadly defined, is the process of interrelating ends and means. When we apply this process to a particular set of ends and means, the product—that is, the strategy—is a specific way of using specified *means* to achieve distinct *ends*. Strategy is thus both a process and a product. Any discussion of ends and means in war must begin with two basic points. First, as we have observed, war is an expression of politics. The ends or goals of any party waging war—even though those goals may be social, economic, religious, or ideological in nature—are by definition political goals. Second, wars are fought by political entities that have unique characteristics and often very dissimilar goals and resources. In order to understand any conflict, we must appreciate the ways in which the means and ends of the participants may vary.

NATIONAL STRATEGY

Our primary interest is in *military strategy*, the art and science of employing the armed forces of a nation to secure the objectives of national policy by the application of force or the threat of force.[2] However, in order to place military strategy in its proper context, it is necessary to understand national strategy. Military strategy is subordinate to *national strategy*, which is the art and science of developing and using political, economic, military, and informational powers, together with armed force, during peace and war, to secure the objectives of policy.[3] Of necessity, we must begin with national strategy and describe how ends and means must be related at the very highest levels before we can proceed to determine military objectives and strategies.

At the highest levels, ends are expressed as national interests. Interests are a nation's wants, needs, and concerns. Specifically, national interests normally involve four main areas: survival and security, political and territorial integrity, economic stability and well-being, and stability. Conflict can arise as a result of a threat (or perceived threat) to any one of these four areas. Interests are central to a discussion of strategy because interests signal a nation's desires and intentions to other nations. As discussed earlier, nation and state are not synonymous.

Certain interests that a nation sees as essential are referred to as *vital* interests. Vital interests are distinguished from other interests by the fact that nations are usually unwilling to compromise on them and are often prepared to resort to conflict in support of them.[4] Thus, when examining a strategic situation, a strategist must identify not only what interests are at stake but also which interests one or more of the participants view as vital.

National interests are often vague or consist of highly generalized abstractions. While national interests underpin national strategy, the specifics of the strategy must focus on more concrete ends. The specific goals and aims of national strategy are often referred to as objectives. Objectives are the ends a nation must achieve to promote, protect, or attain its interests. Objectives tend to be more tangible than interests because they normally describe specific activities or conditions which must be attained. Objectives provide the departure point for national strategy in that they describe what a state is actually trying to do.[5]

In peacetime, national interests and objectives lead to specific policies and commitments. Policy is a pattern or patterns of actions designed to attain specific objectives. Policy can represent a broad course of action or intent. Policy is the ways (methods or patterns) by which strategy reaches its objectives. Commitments are expressions of a nation's intention to use its instruments of national power. Whereas policy might express general intent, a course of action, or restraints on action, commitments pledge nations to take specific actions at specific times and places. While conflict is always related to some national interest or objective, it is normally the outgrowth of a specific policy or commitment.

The articulation of national interests, objectives, policies, and commitments linked to use of the instruments of national power is sometimes referred to as "grand strategy," "grand national strategy," or, currently in the United States, "national security strategy." Grand strategies or national security strategies are implemented by subordinate strategies—political or diplomatic strategies, economic strategies, national military strategies, and so forth—for the use of each of the instruments of national power.

Knowledge of this peacetime strategic framework (figure 1) is required in order to comprehend the origins of any particular conflict situation. However, it is even more important to understand the links among national strategy, military strategy, and other supporting strategies during conflict. Without this fundamental understanding, it will be difficult to establish the appropriate relationship between policy and the military action intended to carry out the policy.

In war, the national strategy focuses the instruments of national power[6] on achieving its political ends or objectives as

Figure 1. Relationship of political objectives to national strategy and supporting strategies.

articulated by the political leadership. Diplomatic, economic, military, and informational actions are linked through supporting strategies that contribute to attaining the objective of national strategy.

Military strategy, in turn, applies the military instrument of national power towards the accomplishment of the political objectives of the overall national strategy. The departure point for military strategy, therefore, is the objectives of the national strategy. From there, military strategy must identify a military goal or objective that will lead to accomplishment of the political objective. The military objective then provides the basis for the identification of specific ways to accomplish that objective. The selection of one of these courses of action and its further development results in a strategic concept that embodies the key components of the chosen military strategy. The military strategy is not developed in isolation from the other instruments of national power. The military objectives and strategy must also be compatible with the diplomatic, economic, and informational objectives and strategies.

Strategists must be able to analyze the overall strategic situation and appreciate the larger context in which military strategy is executed. In order to formulate and implement an effective military strategy, they must understand the ends and means of the larger national strategy as well as the strategies of the enemy, allies, and related neutral parties. In order to develop this understanding, we now look more deeply at ends and means within national strategy.

ENDS IN NATIONAL STRATEGY

Survival and Victory

There are only two fundamental national strategic goals in any conflict: survival and victory. Any specific aims that we may pursue will reflect one or both of these two goals. Survival is the minimum goal of opponents and a prerequisite for victory. Victory is normally associated with the achievement of the political aims of the war, but it also requires an end to the war and the reestablishment of peace. The strategist must strive to understand what survival and victory mean in the specific situation at hand to *each* of the struggle's par- ticipants.

Survival is the continued existence of the political entity that is at war. However, survival can mean different things to different political entities. Survival often equates to the continuance of a way of life or the well-being of the population. Threats to this type of survival are usually met with fierce resistance. Sometimes the survival of a particular individual or group will take priority over the interests of the whole. In such a case, strategies that seek to compel submission by threatening the interests of the nation or of its people may have little direct impact. Finally, some political groups or ideological movements are willing to fight on until they are destroyed. Their hopes of survival lie in leaving behind a heroic legend to influence future generations or in making some other kind of lasting statement to humanity or God. For these groups, even the threat of annihilation may have little impact on their actions.

Victory can be as hard to define as survival. Victory normally means the accomplishment of the specific political aims for which the group went to war. In practice, however, victory may mean merely ending the war on terms less unfavorable to oneself than to the enemy. If the costs of continuing a military struggle come to exceed the value of the goal, meaningful victory is unattainable. Given the nature of war, however, such cost-benefit analysis is more easily described than accomplished. A major problem with victory as a goal is that victory is an emotion-laden word. The accomplishment of limited military and political aims that do not satisfy the emotions or seem to justify the costs of the war may not *feel* like victory. Because we cannot precisely measure the value of most wars aims or accurately judge the cost of their attainment, it is often difficult to perceive the point at which the cost of fighting exceeds the value of victory.

The main point in this discussion of survival and victory is that the problem of identifying what survival and victory mean to various participants in war can be extremely difficult. Our analysis must involve a multitude of considerations that are different in every conflict.

Political Objectives

Political entities go to war for a variety of reasons, ranging from the simple, such as seizing or protecting a valuable piece of territory, to the abstract such as "defending national honor" or "maintaining the balance of power." Despite their diversity, political objectives in war can be labeled as either *limited* or *unlimited*. The distinction is fundamental. An unlimited political objective amounts to the elimination of the opponent as a political entity. A limited political objective, on the other hand, is one in which the enemy leadership can survive and remain in power. See figure 2.

When a political entity seeks an unlimited political objective, its enemy's leadership is to be removed (perhaps merely deposed, perhaps exiled, imprisoned, or executed), while the

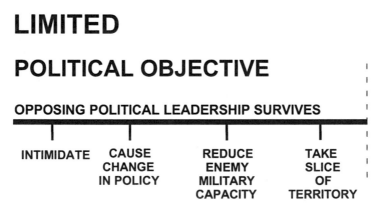

Figure 2. Limited and unlimited
political objectives.

enemy's former assets (territory, population, economic resources) may be absorbed, redistributed, or eradicated. Ab-
sorption can mean many things. With the breakup of
Yugoslavia, Serbia began an effort to systematically reabsorb
each of the newly established states with the intent to reestab-
lish a new Yugoslavia under Serbian control. On the other
hand, the United States' invasion of Panama successfully dis-
posed of the current regime but upon reconstitution left the
Panamanian people in control of their government. Both cases
provide examples of unlimited political objectives. The first
demonstrates the desire to remove the current leadership and
absorb territory, population, and resources. The second demonstrates the desire to remove the current leadership and redis-
tribute the sources of power.

UNLIMITED

POLITICAL OBJECTIVE

OPPOSING POLITICAL LEADERSHIP IS REMOVED

| CHANGE REGIME | CHANGE FORM OF GOVERNMENT/ RULING CLASS | CONQUER/ ABSORB | EXTERMINATE (GENOCIDE) |

Figure 2. Limited and unlimited
political objectives—Continued.

45

An unlimited political objective, then, may embrace anything from merely deposing a particular leader to physically exterminating an entire people or culture. Ideological revolutionaries, would-be world conquerors, and both sides in most true civil wars[7] tend to seek unlimited political objectives. Occasionally, defensive alliances seeking to eliminate a habitual aggressor will also pursue an unlimited political objective.

Conversely, a limited political objective includes anything short of eliminating the political opponent. It is envisioned that the enemy leadership will remain in control after the conclusion of hostilities, although some aspects of its power (influence, territory, resources, or internal control) will be reduced or curtailed. Limited political objectives are characteristic of states seeking better positions in the international balance of power, clans vying for political position within a larger society, mafias or street gangs battling for "turf," and reformist political movements.

MEANS IN NATIONAL STRATEGY

In the purest sense, the means in war is combat—physically attacking the enemy or defending against his attacks upon us. However, war is not limited to purely military means. In fact, military means are only one element used to implement a national strategy. The relative importance placed on the military element of the national strategy varies greatly depending on the nature and the particular circumstances of the struggle. *All* of the instruments of power—diplomatic, economic, military, and informational—must be brought to bear and exploited to the fullest in war.

Diplomacy is the art of employing communications and establishing relationships in the global environment. Ideas, prestige, and commitment are the currencies of the field. The diplomatic instrument uses a nation's international position combined with diplomacy to achieve national objectives. Diplomatic tools may include negotiations, political recognition, treaties, and alliances. While the diplomatic instrument is normally emphasized before hostilities actually begin, it remains a key element of the national strategy in any conflict situation. In certain situations (especially military operations other than war), the diplomatic instrument continues to be the main effort, even after the commitment of military forces.

The economic instrument uses the application of material resources to achieve national objectives. Nations employ economic means to protect their own industries and markets, to improve the quality of life of their people, to stabilize the economy and government of friends and allies, and to deter destabilizing and hostile actions by other nations. Specific economic means include regulation of trade practices, loans and loan guarantees, monetary and investment policies, foreign aid, subsidies, and technology transfers. As with the diplomatic instrument, the economic instrument generally has primacy over the military instrument during peace and is often used before military force during a crisis; changes in trade or monetary policy, economic sanctions, or some type of embargo are frequently the first steps taken in an effort to influence an adversary's behavior. However, economic considerations continue to be at the forefront of any conflict, and the use of economic measures to support the friendly war effort and to undermine the enemy's ability to resist continue throughout the course of a war.

The military instrument is the use of force or the threat to use force to achieve national objectives. Military power is the sum of a nation's weapons and equipment, trained manpower, organizations, doctrines, industrial base, and sustainment capacity. The military instrument can be employed in a variety of ways that are short of combat such as training allies, establishing presence, or acting as a show-of-force. However, the main use of military power is in conflict. While the military instrument is often the main effort during war, the nature and objectives of the particular conflict must be examined to determine the appropriate relationship between the use of military force and the application of the other instruments of national power.

The informational instrument (previously known as the psychological element or instrument) refers to the use of information and ideas to advance the interests and achieve the objectives of the nation. The objective in the use of the information instrument is to influence the perceptions and attitudes of allies, adversaries, and interested observers. Informational tools include the expression of intent and motive, propaganda and press releases, information and personalities, food drops and medical care for refugees—in short, anything that affects the rational or emotional components of the human mind.

While less tangible than the others, the power of ideas and information is real and should not be underestimated. With the informational instrument, a nation can create a psychological impact causing responses ranging from awe or admiration to fear or loathing. This psychological impact can influence not only political and military leaders but the societies of the nations involved and world opinion. It can generate sympathy or antipathy inspired by the culture, ideas, values, and stated cause and objectives for which the parties are fighting.

The instruments of national power overlap and interconnect. Diplomats' power to sway other governments is greatly dependent on those governments' awareness of economic and military power and on their assessment of a nation's willingness to use that power. Economic power is bolstered by military power that can defend economic interests. Military power is often dependent on the diplomats' ability to gain basing rights and overflight permission from other countries or to enlist them in alliances and coalitions. Military power is directly dependent on the financial and technological strength of the nation's economy.

Military professionals naturally concentrate on the military means of strategy, but they should also be conscious of the other means that can be exploited and must be defended in the larger political struggle. Most importantly, they must understand that *military force is an inappropriate tool for the solution of most political difficulties.* Force is at best a necessary means for clearing obstacles to more peaceful solutions. This appreciation of the role of force is a vital component of military professionalism, for military leaders have a responsibility to ensure that political leaders understand both the capabilities and the limitations of the military instrument.

In appraising the relationship between the military and non-military instruments of our national power in any given situation, we must be prepared to ask:

- How can our military capabilities complement or assist the other instruments of national power in achieving our political goals?

- How can diplomatic, informational, and economic instruments of our national power aid our military efforts?

- How might our uses of force impede or imperil the achievement of our political goals?

We must seek to achieve our goals as economically as possible and with the right combination of means—diplo- matic, economic, military, and informational. The way in which we combine these means in any given conflict will be greatly affected by the kind of strategy we pursue and by the strategic goals we seek.

ADAPTING ENDS TO MEANS, AND VICE VERSA

When discussing strategy in the abstract, we often treat means and ends as fixed. In practice, however, we frequently adjust both. The occurrences of war—successes and failures, lessons learned, new ideas, the entry of new combatants—may cause us to shift both our means and our goals. As our resources increase, as we gain confidence in our abilities, and as we find our enemy more vulnerable than we had imagined, we tend to expand our goals. On the other hand, when we find our resources or abilities inadequate, we cut our ambitions to match.

Given time, determination, and creativity, means can be developed to achieve many reasonable goals. Means are adjustable to some degree at every level. Moreover, our ends can affect the means available to us. War aims that evoke popular enthusiasm can give leaders access to resources otherwise unavailable. The emotions created by violence can help war to feed itself, as it energizes people to greater efforts and sacrifices than would be otherwise obtainable.

Another example of the different ways strategic means can be adjusted to match strategic ends can be found in the shifting American strategy of the Cold War. From the Truman administration on, the American government pursued the goal of

51

containing the Soviet Union. The means adopted, however, tended to shift from administration to administration.[8]

President Eisenhower's administration employed a strategy labeled "massive retaliation," which relied on the United States' nuclear superiority to deter Soviet expansion. The Soviet Union possessed huge conventional forces but could not match the American nuclear capability. Eisenhower wished to avoid building and maintaining large conventional forces, arguing that nuclear weapons provided "more bang for the buck." Rather than attempt to match the Soviet's conventional military power, massive retaliation threatened a nuclear response to any aggressive move by the Soviet Union.

Although containment remained the broad goal, President Kennedy's following administration had an entirely different approach to means. The strategic situation was changing to some extent because of the very success of the earlier massive retaliation strategy. The Soviets' nuclear arsenal was growing, and they had found a way around the American nuclear umbrella by sponsoring numerous "wars of national liberation." It became necessary to confront the Soviets with conventional and counterinsurgency forces as well as with nuclear arms. The Kennedy administration formulated the strategy of "flexible response," requiring forces capable of deterring and, if necessary, fighting the Soviets at all levels of conflict.

The resources and commitments necessary to carry out "flexible response" proved too costly for the Nation, and President Nixon's administration again changed the means used to pursue the goal of containment. The strategy of détente was intended to convince the Soviets to restrain themselves based upon a combination of pressures and induce- ments. Among these pressures and inducements were the conduct of direct negotiations with the Soviet Union on issues such as arms control, the establishment of links to the People's Republic of China, and a new set of policies toward United States' allies which has been called "the Nixon doctrine." The Nixon doctrine emphasized establishment of a series of bilateral and multilateral alliances to contain Soviet expansion. The United States would provide economic and military support to its allies, many of whom bordered on the Soviet Union or one of its clients. Military aid consisted primarily of air and naval support along with the implicit protection offered by the United States' nuclear capabilities. As a result of the United States' experience in Vietnam, however, the commitment of United States' ground units would occur only in cases of long-standing treaty obligations such as in Western Europe or Korea.

ENDS IN MILITARY STRATEGY

Just as a national strategy will have a number of political objectives, a particular military strategy will have a number of specific military objectives. However, there are only two fundamental ends behind the use of military force. The first is to physically overpower the enemy's military capacity, leaving him unable to resist our demands. The other is to inflict such high costs on the enemy that he is willing to negotiate an end to hostilities on the terms we desire. The first of these alternatives represents what we call a strategy of *annihilation.*[9] In an annihilation strategy, our military objective is unlimited: we seek to eliminate the enemy's ability to resist, thus leaving him helpless to oppose the imposition of our will. The second alternative is a strategy of *erosion.*[10] Here, our military objective is limited: we seek only to raise the enemy's costs so high that he will find ending the war on our terms more attractive than continuing to fight.

The goal of a strategy of annihilation is to deprive the enemy of the ability to resist, to make him militarily helpless. Annihilation does not require the complete physical destruction of the enemy's military forces. Rather, it requires that the forces be so demoralized and disorganized that they become unable to effectively interfere with the achievement of our political goals. What is being annihilated—literally "made into nothing"—is the enemy's physical means to oppose us.

Normally, a strategy of annihilation is viable only when one of the participants possesses some very great superiority over the other in terms of brute strength, military skill, leadership, technological capabilities, or morale. Without such an advantage, annihilation strategies often fail, resulting in protracted conflicts and requiring such a commitment of resources that one or all the parties find themselves exhausted before the enemy can be eliminated. The 1980-1988 Iran-Iraq War and the

Bosnian conflict from 1992 to 1995 are representative examples of what happens when states pursue annihilation strategies without the necessary advantages. Sometimes the necessary superiority can be obtained through surprise, although this is hard to achieve and dangerous to rely on. If the opponent has any strategic depth, he may recover from his surprise before victory is assured.

The objective of the second approach—a strategy of erosion—is to convince the enemy that settling the political dispute will be easier and the outcome more attractive than continued conflict. To put it another way, erosion strategies seek to present the enemy with the probability of an outcome worse *in his eyes* than peace on the adversary's terms. This is accomplished through eroding or wearing down the enemy's will to fight, rather than destroying his ability to resist.

Erosion strategies are used to pursue a limited political objective when one combatant is either unable or unwilling to destroy the opponent's war-making capability. In many cases, an erosion strategy is required simply because the enemy is too powerful or difficult to annihilate. In other cases, this approach is used because one party does not want or need to destroy the other's military capacity. Perhaps the goal requires such a modest concession from the enemy that it is reasonable to believe he will acquiesce after modest resistance. In another example, there may be a continuing need to keep the opponent's military forces in existence as a buffer or as a factor in the balance of power.

Relationship Between Political and Military Objectives

Political objectives and military objectives are very different things. Political objectives describe, in a sense, where we want to go. Military objectives describe what we have to accomplish militarily in order to get there.

If the political objective is unlimited, the military strategy must be unlimited. Conversely, a limited political objective may call for a military strategy with limited objectives—that is, an erosion strategy. In Afghanistan, the Mujahidin and their Western backers sought a limited political objective: to get the Soviet Union to withdraw from the struggle. Accordingly, they pursued an erosion strategy, seeking to make the Afghan adventure too costly for the Soviet government to sustain.

Though our political objective is limited, it does not necessarily follow that our military strategy must also be limited (figure 3). The Gulf War provides an example of an unlimited military strategy applied successfully in pursuit of a limited political objective. The Coalition had a limited political objective: restore Kuwait's independence. In order to attain this objective, however, it was necessary to destroy all capability of the Iraqi forces to resist and forcibly eject them from Kuwait. Thus, the Coalition employed a strategy of annihilation, pursuing the total defeat of Iraq's military capacity within the Kuwait theater of operations.

56

Strategies of annihilation are conceptually simple. The focus of operational efforts is the enemy's armed forces and the object is to render them powerless. Those forces may be annihilated through battle or through destruction of the social or industrial infrastructure that supports them. The main effort is the armed forces. The diplomatic, economic, and informational instruments of national power support the military effort. Victory is easily measured: when one side's fighting forces are no longer able to present organized resistance, the other side has won.

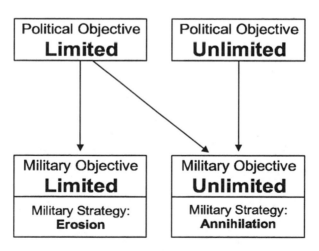

Figure 3. Relationship between political and military objectives.

By comparison, erosion strategies involve many more variables. In erosion strategies, there is a much wider choice in the designation of a main effort among the instruments of national power, the relationship of military force to the other instruments of power, and the definition of victory. Attacks may be focused on the enemy's armed forces, as in an annihilation strategy, or some other valuable resource such as territory, commerce, or financial assets may be seized, threatened, or neutralized. Military forces are normally the main effort in the seizing and holding of territory. Successful embargoes and the freezing of financial assets, on the other hand, often depend primarily on diplomatic and economic power. It may also be possible to undermine an enemy's domestic or international political position through the use of informational or psychological operations.

Victory in a strategy of erosion can be more flexibly defined or more ambiguous than is the case with an annihilation strategy. The enemy's submission to our demands may be explicit or implicit, embodied in a formal treaty or in behind-the-scenes agreements. Convinced that we have made our point, we may simply "declare victory and go home." A compromise may allow both sides to claim success. Victories in erosion strategies thus tend to be undramatic, but they can have tremendous political consequences. The West's success in its containment of the Communist bloc, essentially a very long-term erosion strategy, offers a powerful example.

**Distinguishing Between Erosion
and Annihilation Strategies**

Although annihilation and erosion are conceptually quite different, in practice it is often hard to distinguish between them.
There are several reasons for this ambiguity. First, annihilation
and erosion become practically indistinguishable when one side
or both pursue annihilation, but neither has an overwhelming
military superiority. In such a case, unlimited political and
military objectives can be obtained only through "slugging it
out." This guarantees roughly comparable losses on both sides
and can lead to negotiated settlements, even though one or both
sides originally sought unlimited ob- jectives.

Second, these two strategies can overlap, or one can lead to
the other. Sometimes it is the *threat* of annihilation that forces
the enemy to make a deal. In that case, the difference between
an erosion strategy and one of annihilation is that the enemy is
offered an option of settling the issue before he is made helpless. Conversely, if an enemy cannot be worn down through an
erosion strategy into accepting a settlement, it may be necessary to switch to a strategy of annihilation.

Third, a strategy that has not yet fully taken shape may be
ambiguous. In some cases, this ambiguity reflects calculation:
either the strategy is decided but is being disguised, or the
strategist has goals that can be fulfilled via either approach and
is waiting to see how his opportunities develop. In other cases,
ambiguity reflects poor strategy making: the strategy maker
does not know what he wants to achieve or how to achieve it.

59

Ultimately, however, a successful strategy must turn out to be one or the other. At war's end, a strategy that has neither eliminated the enemy's ability to resist nor worn down his will to continue the struggle is a strategy that has failed.

The distinction between strategies of annihilation and erosion is fundamental. The successful strategist must be able to distinguish which strategy is being pursued or should be pursued in a given situation. The ability to determine which strategy is appropriate in turn depends upon the strategist's understanding of the ends of national strategy and the means employed to achieve those ends. Without this foundation, it is impossible to arrive at the specifics of a particular military strategy: the determination of military objectives, the identification of the appropriate means to achieve those objectives, and the development of the strategic concept.

Chapter 3

Strategic Opposites

"Grand strategy must always remember that peace follows war."[1]

—B. H. Liddell Hart

I t is crucial to distinguish between annihilation and erosion strategies and to understand who is pursuing which goal and why. There are, however, a great many other dimensions to any strategic situation. The dynamics of a struggle are affected not only by the differing political and military goals of the antagonists but by similarities and differences in their character, the kinds of forces they employ, the techniques they use, and the ways they see—and are seen by—the world. In making a strategic assessment, such factors are more important than a simple numerical comparison of units and equipment.

In this chapter, we will examine several sets of strategic opposites that are helpful in understanding the nature of the strategic problem. All of these pairs of opposites do not necessarily apply to every strategic situation, nor do these approaches necessarily influence each other. For example, whether a strategy is symmetrical or asymmetrical has little bearing on whether it is annihilative or erosive. Nonetheless, a grasp of these concepts will help us to formulate the questions we must ask as we try to understand the specific problem before us.

DEFENSIVE AND OFFENSIVE STRATEGIES

The strategic attacker is the antagonist seeking to add to his relative power. It usually is the side that initiates a war, although defenders sometimes launch preemptive attacks. An attacker may be seeking to completely overthrow the balance of power or may simply want an upward adjustment in his relative position. This distinction affects the kinds of strategies both sides pursue and the intensity of the struggle.

The strategic defender is the participant that wants to keep what he has or to maintain his relative position in a balance of power system. In many important respects, defense is inherently stronger than offense. The strength of the strategic defense derives from human psychology and the balance of power mechanism as well as the forces of friction and inertia. People are naturally willing to endure great sacrifices in defense of their homes and homelands and much less willing to endure such sacrifices in military adventures abroad. An aggressor's action frequently causes anxiety and hostility in neighboring allied and neutral countries; they often interpret a challenge to the existing balance of power as a threat and are more naturally inclined to support the defender. Friction and inertia are normally on the side of the defender as well: it is inherently easier to hold onto something than to take it away from someone else.

These political and psychological strengths of the strategic defense are present in all wars, even those in which territorial gains and losses are not a major factor. The strength of the defense is often reinforced operationally since the attacker is normally moving away from his base of supply and the center of his political power, while the defender is falling back on his.

Note, of course, that this superiority of the strategic defense is not an absolute. Obviously, a defender with few resources and poor leadership is not stronger than an attacker with vastly greater resources and good leadership. However, all other things being equal, the defender has the advantage.

At the tactical and operational levels, the roles of attacker and defender may frequently change hands or even be shared more or less evenly. At the strategic level, however, the roles tend to be fixed throughout any given conflict. In World War II, for instance, the Western Allies held the advantages of the strategic defense even as their armies marched into Germany. They were perceived as being restorers of the balance of power rather than as threats to it. However, in some situations, the roles of strategic attacker and defender can be reversed. When war is endemic in a society, when the origins of the conflict are poorly remembered, or when the war guilt has come to be equally shared, the advantages of the original defender tend to be lost. In such a case, the balance of power mechanism usually tends to support the current defender and to oppose whichever contender seems momentarily to have the initiative.

SYMMETRICAL AND ASYMMETRICAL STRATEGIES

Strategies can be either symmetrical or asymmetrical. That is, the contending powers may pursue mirror-image ends or rely on similar means, or they may pursue quite different kinds of goals or apply dissimilar means.[2]

A symmetrical military strategy is one that attempts to match—or rather, to overmatch—the enemy strength for strength, to beat him on his own terms. An asymmetrical strategy is one that attempts to apply one category of means against another category, to use some means to which the enemy cannot effectively respond in kind.

Many wars are fought between very different enemies and are thus profoundly asymmetrical in character. For example, a terrorist organization may wage war against a government or even against the international community as a whole. The terrorist campaigns of the Irish Republican Army against the United Kingdom and the Palestine Liberation Organization against Israel are illustrations. Most states would like nothing better than for terrorists to act symmetrically and resort to open battle, which would make them vulnerable to the state's superior conventional military forces. On the other hand, terrorists may also seek to provoke a symmetrical response: the purpose of many terrorist attacks is to provoke governments into actions that antagonize ordinary citizens such as restrictive security measures or even reprisals in kind. These acts undermine the legitimacy and credibility of the government and play into the hands of the terrorist strategy. Because of the fundamentally different natures of the adversaries, the political effects of these similar actions are dramatically different.

Most real-world strategies are a mixture of symmetrical and asymmetrical elements, and it is often difficult to determine the overall balance between them. Thus any discussion of symmetry or asymmetry in war is a matter of degree as well as kind. The usefulness of the concept is that it helps us analyze the dynamics of a struggle. For example, the American strategy of containment during the Cold War always involved strong elements of both symmetry and asymmetry. From a military standpoint, Eisenhower's massive retaliation policy was fundamentally an asymmetrical strategy: the United States would reply to any type of Soviet aggression "by means and at places of our own choosing."[3] This was generally interpreted to mean a U.S. nuclear response to a conventional Soviet provocation. From the national strategic standpoint however, Eisenhower's strategy was broadly similar to the Soviet Union's in that both relied primarily on deterrence rather than on the actual application of military force. The Kennedy administration's subsequent flexible response strategy was militarily a symmetrical strategy of matching the Soviets strength for strength. However, it also took advantage of economic and political asymmetries.

There is no innate advantage or disadvantage to either a symmetrical or asymmetrical strategy. The choice depends on the situation and on the constraints of time and creativity. The interplay between symmetry and asymmetry in any struggle is unique and covers a wide range of possibilities. In India's post-World War II struggle for independence, for example, British military power was overthrown by the most asymmetrical approach imaginable: Gandhi's campaign of nonvio- lence.

A particular strategy must take into account the similarities and differences between the opponents and must—when necessary or advantageous—seek to create new ones. The effective strategist is not biased in favor of either symmetry or asymmetry but is keenly aware of both and of the interplay between them.

DETERRENCE: STRATEGIES OF REPRISAL OR DENIAL

Deterrence means dissuading an enemy from an action by means of some countervailing threat. There are essentially two methods of deterrence: denial and reprisal.

To deter by denial means to prevent an enemy's action by convincing him that his action will fail. Conceptually, this is a symmetrical approach (although the actual means of denial may be either symmetrical or asymmetrical). For example, a state may deter conventional invasion by maintaining sufficiently credible forces to defend its borders. It may deter the use of poison gas by training and equipping its forces and population to function effectively in a chemical warfare environment. Terrorists may be deterred from attacks on airports by tight security.

The second approach, reprisal, is conceptually asymmetrical. We may concede to the enemy that he is capable of taking what he wants from us but seek to convince him that his prize will not be worth the price he will pay for it. For example, a state weak in conventional forces may seek to deter enemy occupation by credibly preparing to wage a long, painful guerrilla war of resistance. Conventional invasion might also be deterred through the threat of nuclear retaliation.

There are overlaps between denial and reprisal. Tight airport security may deter terrorists by convincing them either that their efforts will fail (denial) or that they will be caught and punished (reprisal). A demonstrated capability to wage chemical warfare may deter a gas attack both by denying the enemy an advantage and by threatening to retaliate in kind.

As these examples indicate, in practice denial and reprisal are often more effective when applied in tandem. The ability of one side to deny its enemy an advantage cannot always be absolutely convincing, especially if the other side is inclined to take risks. Deterrence by denial also implies a certain passivity. An enemy may be willing to test the defenses if he believes that

69

failure carries no further penalty. On the other hand, while deterrence by reprisal compensates for some of the weakness of denial, reprisal has its own weaknesses. Retaliation, even if carried out successfully, may come too late to avoid suffering significant damage.

STANDARDIZED OR TAILORED STRATEGIES

Usually, when we talk about the conscious formulation of a particular strategy, we are talking about a specific way of using specific means to reach specific ends. This is a strategy "tailored" to deal with a particular problem. Our means are finely adapted to fit our ends, and vice versa.

There are classes of problems, however, that do not initially lend themselves to such tailoring. These problems usually fall

- First, we lack the time to tailor a unique response to a specific problem. This can be the case in rapidly unfolding strategic problems or when we are unwilling or unable to adapt for some other reason.

- Second, we lack the specific knowledge needed to craft a unique strategy but recognize the problem as fitting a certain pattern.

In such cases, we normally adopt a standardized strategy, whether or not it is truly appropriate to the specific problem.

Standardized and tailored strategies are not mutually exclusive. Often a standardized strategy provides the point of departure for a tailored strategy that evolves as the situation develops. If we run into certain types of problems often enough, we develop standardized responses that are generally appropriate to that type of problem. Experience has taught us they will work more often than not. In many cases, standardized strategies are designed to gain time to find an appropriate, specific solution.

Standardized strategies are not fixed; they can be changed and improved, usually on the basis of experience. These strategies build a certain reputation that may strongly influence the behavior of friends, foes, and neutrals. Standardized strategies generally find expression not within a single war, but over the course of many conflicts. Such a strategy's immediate payoff in any particular case may be less than completely satisfying, but it can offer great advantages over the long term.

As an example, the United States has employed a standardized strategy of providing nation-building support to defeated enemies. During the period of reconstruction, the United States assists in rebuilding the defeated states' industrial base and infrastructure. Two notable examples are the recon- struction of Germany and Japan following World War II. More recently, the United States provided postconflict aid to Grenada, Panama, and Haiti.

In its conduct of war, the United States pursues a standard strategy that includes respect for the independence of allies, relatively mild occupation policies, the generous and systematic reconstruction of conquered states, as well as a persistent economic isolation of hostile nations. These policies reflect a recognition that wars end and that the victors must live with the survivors. This approach also makes it easier for other states to act as American allies and difficult for enemies to create and sustain popular resistance to American power and influence. Combined with the American reputation for overwhelming firepower and a demonstrated willingness to use it in war, such policies have contributed greatly to America's strategic success.

STRATEGY BY INTENT OR BY DEFAULT

Not all strategies are the product of conscious thought. Warfare is driven by politics, and rational calculation is only one of many factors in politics. Strategies by intent are those developed primarily through the rational consideration of options and their likely implications. Strategies by default, on the other hand, are those dictated by circumstances or determined primarily by ideologies, unconscious assumptions, and prejudices that prevent strategists from considering all of their options in what many would consider a fully rational manner. While conceptually distinct, the two are rarely mutually exclusive; most strategies involve elements of both intent and default.

Consider the Russian strategic response to invasion by Germany in World War II. The Russian intent was to defend their country at the border. The strength of their enemy forced the Russians into a strategy of delay and withdrawal until the invader could be worn down sufficiently to be defeated. Conversely, the Nazis' blind adherence to their racial ideologies led to their failure to take advantage of the indifferent attitudes of the Belorussian and Ukrainian peoples towards the Soviet regime. Had they pursued a rational policy towards the population of occupied Soviet territory, they might have undermined the growth of a powerful partisan movement behind their lines.

The functioning of coalitions offers another illustration of the interplay between strategies of intent and default. Coalition warfare is often entered into as part of an intentional strategy. However, strategies adopted by the coalition are complicated or even subverted by the ideological motivations of the participants. Dictatorships generally have difficulty participating in coalition warfare. However sensible it might be to cooperate with other political entities in pursuit of common goals, dictatorships by their very nature demand the right to make decisions unilaterally. They attempt to treat potential allies as servants, subordinating others' interests completely to their own. Theocratic states that find their justification for existence in the demands of God may have a similar difficulty in making rational strategic compromises. Liberal democracies that are cooperative, compromising, balance-of-power entities internally are much more likely than dictatorships or theocracies to demonstrate these same characteristics in their external relationships. They are also more likely to attempt to treat very different kinds of political entities as if they shared those values.

What we have described are only tendencies. Insightful and strong-willed leaders occasionally overcome such tendencies. Strategists must seek to understand which elements of their own and the enemy's strategies are fixed by nature and which are subject to conscious change. A policy that seeks to convince the enemy to change his behavior will fail if he is incapable of change.

EVALUATING OPPOSING STRATEGIES

The purpose of presenting the sets of opposing strategies in this chapter is analytical rather than prescriptive. We must use these concepts to understand what we, our allies, our enemies, and relevant neutral forces are doing and why. They deepen our understanding and throw new light on sometimes inscrutable opponents. Faced with the possibility of war, however, the strategist must return to the fundamentals we described in chapter 2: *What are the political objectives of each participant? Are they limited or unlimited? How do the oppo-nents perceive each other's objectives?* The answers to these questions will have implications for the fundamental character of any resulting conflict and the adoption of a particular strat-egy. We must appreciate which elements of the situation are fixed and which are subject to conscious change. We must be prepared to deal with the constants and norms as well as uncer-tainty and ambiguity. Only then can we intelligently discuss the strategy-making process, as we do in the following chapter.

Chapter 4

The Making
of
Strategy

"Modern warfare resembles a spider's web—everything connects, longitudinally or laterally, to everything else; there are no 'independent strategies,' no watertight compartments, nor can there be."[1]

—John Terraine

Having considered the nature of the environment within which strategy is made, the fundamental goals of all strategies, and some ways to categorize a strategy, we now consider how strategy is actually made.

THE STRATEGY-MAKING PROCESS

Despite all that we have said about the nature of politics and policy, people generally think of strategy making as a conscious, rational process—the direct and purposeful interrelating of ends and means. In fact, strategy is very seldom if ever made in a fully rational way.

Each political entity has its own mechanism for developing strategy. While certain elements of the strategy-making process may be clearly visible, specified in a constitution and law or conducted in open forum, many aspects of the process are difficult to observe or comprehend. Participants in the process itself may not fully understand or even be aware of the dynamics that take place when dealing with a specific strategic situation. Thus, it is impossible to define any sort of universal strategy-making process. It is possible, however, to isolate certain key elements that any strategy maker must take into account to arrive at a suitable solution to a particular problem. We must focus on these elements if we are to understand the strategy and strategic context of any particular conflict.

Strategy making is in effect a problem-solving process. In order to solve a particular problem, the strategist must understand its nature and identify potential solutions. We start with the nature of the problem and the particular political ends of each of the participants in the conflict. This helps us to identify the specific political objectives to be accomplished. These objectives lead to development of a national strategy to achieve them. From there, we proceed to military strategy.

While it is difficult to specify in advance the content of a military strategy, it is easier to describe the questions that military strategy must answer. First, we must understand the political objectives and establish those military objectives that enable us to accomplish the political objectives. Second, we must determine how best to achieve these military objectives. Finally, we must translate the solution into a specific strategic concept: Will our strategy result in the requirement for multiple theaters or multiple campaigns? What are the intermediate goals and objectives within these theaters and campaigns that will achieve our political objectives? The military strategic concept incorporates the answers to these questions and provides the direction needed by military commanders to implement the strategy.

The Strategic Assessment

When confronted with a strategic problem, strategists must first make an assessment of the situation confronting them. This assessment equates to the observation-orientation steps of the observation-orientation-decide-act loop.[2] While the factors involved and the time constraints at the strategic level are different from those at the tactical or operational levels, the principle is the same: without a basic understanding of the situation, decisionmaking and action are likely to be seriously flawed.

The assessment begins with observing and orienting to the strategic landscape. Strategists look at the factors discussed in chapter 1: the physical environment, national character, the interplay between the states, and balance of power considerations. Once they have an appreciation for the landscape, they must focus on and determine the nature of the conflict.

Assessing the nature of the conflict requires consideration of questions like these: What value do both sides attach to the political objectives of the war? What costs are both sides willing to pay? What is the result of the "value compared to cost" equation? What material, economic, and human sacrifices will the participants endure? For how long? Under what circumstances? Will the societies expect regular, measurable progress? Will they patiently endure setbacks and frustration?

Such questions are fundamentally related to the ends of the conflict and the means employed to achieve those ends. The answers to these questions are required to determine the nature of the political objectives—the ends—of the conflict and the value to both sides of those political objectives. The value of the objective, in turn, is a major indicator of the resources—the means—that both sides will likely commit and the sacrifices they will make to achieve it. An understanding of both ends and means is required in order to develop an effective military strategy.

Political Objectives

Political objectives are the starting point for the development of a strategy. The first step in making strategy is deciding which political objectives a strategy will aim to achieve. In order to design the military action that will produce the desired result, the military strategist needs to know what that desired result is, that is, what the political objective is. From the political objectives, the military strategist can develop a set of military objectives that achieve the political objectives.

In theory, the setting of political objectives seems like a relatively straightforward proposition, and sometimes it is. The World War II stated political objective of unconditional surrender by the Axis powers was simple. In practice, however, setting political objectives involves the solving of not one but several complicated and interrelated problems. Multiple problems require the simultaneous pursuit of mul-tiple and imperfectly meshed—sometimes even conflicting—strategies. The constant pressures and long-term demands of our economic and social strategies tend naturally to conflict with the demands of preparedness for the occasional military emergency. The demands of warfighting, of coalition management, of maintaining domestic unity, and of sustaining the political fortunes of the current leadership often pull us irresistibly in different directions. It is always crucial to remember that military strategy making is but one element of the much broader dynamic of political interaction that goes into the making of national strategy.

At a minimum, the determination of political objectives must establish two things in order to form the basis for the development of a sound military strategy. First, it must establish definitions for both survival and victory for all participants in the conflict. As discussed in chapter 2, without an understanding of how each participant views its survival and victory, it will be impossible to identify the military strategy that can attain either goal. Second, the political leadership must establish whether it is pursuing a limited or unlimited political objective. The identification of the nature of the political objective is essential to ensuring the right match between political and military objectives.

Military Objectives and the Means to Achieve Them

With an understanding of the political objectives, we then turn to selection of our military objectives. Military objectives should achieve or help achieve the political goal of the war. At the same time, the use of military power should not produce unintended or undesirable political results. Fighting the enemy should always be a means to an end, not become an end in itself.

As with political objectives, the choice of military objectives may seem relatively simple. However, selection of military objectives is not a trivial matter. First, strategists may select a military objective that is inappropriate to the political objectives or that does not actually achieve the political objective. Second, there may be more than one way to defeat an enemy. As an example, will it be necessary to defeat the enemy army and occupy the enemy country or might a naval blockade accomplish the objective? Third, the pursuit of some military objectives may change the political goal of the war. Successful pursuit of a particular military objective may have unintentional effects on the enemy, allies, neutrals, and one's own society. This is particularly true in cases where a delicate balance of power is in place; achieving a given military objective may alter the balance of power in such a way that the resulting political situation is actually less favorable to the victor. Successful military strategies select a military goal or goals that secure the desired political objectives, not something else.

The designation of limited or unlimited political objectives is a necessary prerequisite to selecting the type of warfighting strategy that will be employed—either a strategy of annihilation or a strategy of erosion. The choice of an erosion or annihilation strategy drives the selection of specific military objectives, the design of our military actions, the effects we hope to achieve, and the weight we give to our military efforts relative to the use of other elements of our national power.

In annihilation strategies, the military objective is to eliminate the military capacity of the enemy to resist. This almost always involves the destruction of major elements of the enemy's military forces. Attacks against other targets—seizing territory, striking economic capacity, or conducting informational or psychological warfare against the enemy leadership or population—are normally pursued only when they are directly related to degrading or destroying some military capability. Thus, specific military objectives and the means for striking at those military objectives grow out of the assessment of the nature and functioning of the enemy's military capacity.

In contrast, the focus of an erosion strategy is always the mind of the enemy leadership. The aim is to convince the enemy leadership that making concessions offers a better outcome than continuing resistance. The military objectives in an erosion strategy can be similar to those in an annihilation strategy, or they can be considerably different.

The first category of targets in an erosion strategy is the same as in an annihilation strategy: the enemy's armed forces. If the enemy is disarmed or finds the threat to destroy his armed forces credible, he may submit to the conditions presented. On the other hand, certain assets that have limited military importance but are of critical economic or psychological value—a capital city or key seaport—may be seized. Similarly, the enemy's financial assets may be frozen or his trade blockaded. Again, if submission to stated demands is less painful for enemy decisionmakers than continuing to do without the lost asset, they may concede defeat. A third possible target in an erosion strategy is the enemy leadership's domestic political position. Money, arms, and information can be provided to internal opponents of the leadership. The purpose is to make enemy leaders feel so endangered that they will make peace in order to focus on their domestic enemies.

Choosing military objectives and the appropriate means to pursue those objectives requires the consideration of two closely related concepts: the center of gravity and the critical vulnerability.[3]

A center of gravity is a key source of the enemy's *strength*, providing either his physical or his psychological capacity to effectively resist. The utility of the concept is that it forces us to focus on what factors are most important to our enemy in a particular situation and to narrow our attention to as few key factors as possible.

At the strategic level, the range of possible centers of gravity is broad. The enemy's fighting forces may be a center of gravity. Strength may flow from a particular population center, a region providing manpower, or a capital city. A capital city may draw its importance from some practical application such as functioning as a transportation hub or as a command and control nexus. The capital's importance may be cultural, supplying some psychological strength to the population. In the case of nonstate political entities, the source of the enemy's motivation and cohesion may be a key individual or clique or the public perception of the leadership's ideological purity. Public support is often a strategic center of gravity, particularly in democratic societies.

In contrast to a center of gravity, a critical vulnerability is a key potential source of *weakness*. The concept is important because we normally wish to attack an enemy where we may do so with the least danger to ourselves, rather than exposing ourselves directly to his strength. To be *critical*, a vulnerability must meet two criteria: First, the capture, destruction, or exploitation of this vulnerability must significantly undermine or destroy a center of gravity. Second, the critical vulnerability must be something that we have the means to capture, destroy, or exploit.

If the center of gravity is the enemy armed forces, the critical vulnerability may lie in some aspect of its organization or its supporting infrastructure that is both key to the armed forces' functioning and open to attack by means at our disposal. During World War II, the Allies sought to focus on the German armed forces' logistical vulnerabilities by attacking the German petroleum industry, ball bearing supplies, and transportation infrastructure.

As an example of how centers of gravity and critical vulnerabilities are used to determine military objectives and the means to achieve them, consider the North's use of General Winfield Scott's "Anaconda Plan" during the Civil War. The plan identified the South's physical and emotional capacity to sustain a defensive war as one of the strategic centers of gravity. Critical vulnerabilities associated with this strategic center of gravity included the South's small industrial capacity, limited number of seaports, underdeveloped transportation network, and dependence upon foreign sources of supply for foodstuffs, raw materials, and finished goods. The Anaconda Plan targeted this center of gravity by exploiting these vulner-abilities. The plan called for a naval blockade to wall off the Confederacy from trading with Europe, seizure of control of the Mississippi River valley to isolate the South from potential sources of resources and support in Texas and Mexico, and then capture of port facilities and railheads to cut lines of transportation. These actions would gradually reduce the South's military capability to resist as well as undermine popu-lar support for the rebellion. While initially rejected as being too passive, the Anaconda plan revisited and reimplemented, eventually became the general strategy of the North. Scott's experienced analysis of the South's centers of gravity and criti-cal vulnerabilities resulted in an effective military strategy which led directly to the defeat of the Confederacy.[4]

An understanding of centers of gravity and critical vulner-abilities forms the core for the development of a particular military strategy. Among the centers of gravity, strategists find military objectives appropriate to the political objectives and the warfighting strategy being pursued. Among the critical vul-nerabilities, strategists find the most effective and efficient means of achieving those military objectives. Together these concepts help formulate the strategic concept that guides the execution of the military strategy.

Strategic Concepts

An essential step in the making of effective strategy is the development of a strategic concept.[5] Derived from the strategic estimate of the situation and the political and military objectives, this concept describes the course of action to be taken. The strategic concept should provide a clear and compelling basis for all subsequent planning and decisionmaking.

As with the strategy itself, the strategic concept begins with the political objectives. It should identify the military objectives to be accomplished and how to reach them. It should establish the relationship and relative importance of the military means to the other instruments of national power that are being employed. It should address priorities and the allocation of resources. These, in turn should help determine the concentration of effort within a theater or campaign.

Sometimes a war is fought in one theater, sometimes in several. If there is more than one theater, a choice has to be made on how to allocate resources. This cannot be effectively done without some overall idea of how the war will be won. The strategic concept provides this idea. Normally, military objectives are achieved by conducting a number of campaigns or major operations. What should be the objective of a given campaign? Again, it is the strategic concept that answers that question. It gives commanders the guidance to formulate and execute plans for campaigns and major operations.

World War II provides a clear example of the use of the strategic concept. This concept naturally evolved throughout the course of the war. It was modified in response to various political, economic, and military developments and as a result of disagreements among the Allies. It is important to note that the strategic concept was not a single document, but rather a series of decisions made by the leaders of the Alliance. Nevertheless, in this general strategic concept, military leaders could find guidance from their political leadership for the formulation of specific theater strategies and campaign plans.

It was immediately apparent that, given the global scale of the conflict, the strength of the enemy, and the differing political objectives, philosophies, postures, and military capabilities of the Allied nations, a unifying strategy was needed. The strategic concept adopted by the Allies called for the defeat of Germany first, effectively setting the division of labor and establishing priorities between the European and Pacific theaters. As the concept developed, it forced a sequence and priority among the campaigns and operations within theaters and set specific objectives for each of the campaigns. Germany would be engaged through continuous offensive action until a decisive blow could be launched from Britain. Japan would be contained and harassed until sufficient resources were available to go on the offensive in the Pacific. Ultimately, this concept led to the achievement of the military and political objective—in this case, unconditional surrender of Germany and Japan.

WHO MAKES STRATEGY?

Strategy making is almost always a distributed process. The various elements of any particular strategy take shape in various places and at various times and are formed by different leaders and groups motivated by varying concerns. Elements of the strategy eventually adopted may surface anywhere in the organization. We need to understand the particular characteristics, concerns, and goals of all significant participants if we are to understand a specific strategic situation.

Without a detailed examination of the particular political entity and its strategy-making process, it is impossible to determine who is providing the answers to a particular question. Nevertheless, at least in terms of the division between military and civilian decisionmakers, it is possible to identify who should be providing these answers.

Earlier, it was argued that certain questions have to be answered in order to make strategy. The question, *"What is the political objective the war seeks to achieve?"* must be answered by the civilian leadership. The question, *"The attainment of what military objective will achieve, or help achieve, the political objective of the war?"* should also be answered primarily by the political leadership. They alone are in the best position to understand the impact that achievement of the military objective will have on the enemy, allies, neutrals, and

91

domestic opinion. In answering the question, *"How can the military objective be achieved?"* the military leadership comes more to the fore. However, the civilian leadership will want to make sure that the means used to achieve the military objective do not themselves have deleterious effects, effects that may overshadow the political objective of the war. The question, *"If there is more than one theater, how should the war effort be divided among theaters?"* is likely decided primarily by the political leadership, because this question can be answered only with reference to the overall structure of the war. The questions, *"Within a given theater, should the war effort be divided into campaigns?"* and *"What should be the objective of a given campaign?"* would seem to be primarily military in nature. Nevertheless, decisions made here can also affect political objectives or concerns as well as impact on the availability and consumption of scarce human and material resources. No political leader would want to entirely relinquish the decision about what the primary objectives of a campaign should be.

Thus we can see that the making of military strategy is a responsibility shared by both political and military leaders. Military institutions participate in the political process that develops military strategy. The military leadership has a responsibility to advise political leaders on the capabilities, limitations, and best use of the military instrument to achieve the political objectives. Military advice will be meaningless, and political leaders will ignore it unless military professionals understand their real concerns and the political ramifications—both domestic and international—of military action or inaction.

JUST WAR

Traditionally, Western societies have demanded two things of their strategic leaders in war. First is success, which contributes to security and societal well-being. Second is a sense of being in the right, a belief that the cause for which the people are called to sacrifice is a just one. Strategists must be able to reconcile what is *necessary* with what is *just*. The "just war" theory provides a set of criteria that can help to reconcile these practical and moral considerations.

Just war theory has two components, labeled in Latin *jus ad bellum* (literally, "rightness in going to war") and *jus in bello* ("rightness in the conduct of war"). There are seven *jus ad bellum* criteria:[6]

- **Just Cause**. A just cause involves the protection and preservation of value. There are three such causes: defense of self or of others against attack, retaking of something wrongly taken by force, and punishment of concrete wrongs done by an evil power.

- **Right Authority**. The person or body authorizing the war must be a responsible representative of a sovereign political entity.

- **Right Intention**. The intent in waging war must truly be just and not be a selfish aim masked as a just cause.

- **Proportionality of Ends**. The overall good achieved by the resort to war must not be outweighed by the harm it produces.

- **Last Resort**. We must show that there is no logical alternative to violence.

- **Reasonable Hope of Success**. There can be neither moral nor strategic justification for resorting to war when there is no hope of success.

- **The Aim of Peace**. Ends for which a war is fought must include the establishment of stability and peace.

Satisfying just war criteria is often not a simple or clear-cut process. We want to believe in the ethical correctness of our cause. At the same time, we know that our enemies and their sympathizers will use moral arguments against us. Therefore, though the criteria for the rightness in going to war may be met, the translation of political objectives to military objectives and their execution cannot violate *jus in bello*—rightness in the conduct or war. The destruction of a power plant may achieve a tactical or operational objective; however, the impact of its destruction on the civilian populace may violate rightness in conduct and result in loss of moral dignity, adversely affecting overall strategic objectives.

In sum, the just war criteria provide objective measures from which to judge our motives. The effective strategist must be prepared to demonstrate to all sides why the defended cause meets the criteria of just war theory and why the enemy's cause does not. If a legitimate and effective argument on this basis cannot be assembled, then it is likely that both the cause and the strategy are fatally flawed.

STRATEGY-MAKING PITFALLS

Given the complexity of making strategy, it is understandable that some seek ways to simplify the process. There are several traps into which would-be strategists commonly fall: searching for strategic panaceas; emphasizing process over product in strategy making; seeking the single, decisive act, the fait accompli; attempting to simplify the nature of the problem by using labels such as limited or unlimited wars; falling into a paralysis of inaction; or rushing to a conclusion recklessly.

Strategic Panaceas

Strategists have long sought strategic panaceas: strategic prescriptions that will guarantee victory in any situation. The strategic panacea denies any need for understanding the unique characteristics of each strategic situation, offering instead a ready-made and universal solution.

Examples abound. In the 1890s, the American naval writer Alfred Thayer Mahan convinced many world leaders of the validity of his theories centered on capital ships and concentrated battle fleets.[7] These theories prompted Germany to challenge Great Britain for naval dominance, contributing to the tension between the two countries prior to the outbreak of World War I. Similarly, the theories of German Field Marshal Alfred von Schlieffen fixated on strategies of annihilation and battles of envelopment. These prescriptive theories dominated Germany's strategic thinking in both World Wars. The deterrence strategies embraced by American Cold War theorists were equally influential. American forces accordingly designed for high-intensity warfare in Europe proved inap-propriate to counter Communist-inspired wars of national liberation.

Emphasizing Process Over Product

The second major trap is the attempt to reduce the strategy-making process to a routine. The danger in standardizing strategy-making procedures is that the leadership may believe that the process alone will ensure development of sound strategies. Just as there is no strategic panacea, there is no optimal strategy-making process. Nonetheless, political organizations, bureaucracies, and military staffs normally seek to systematize strategy making. These processes are designed to control the collection and flow of information, to standardize strategy making, and to ensure the consistent execution of policy.

Such systems are vitally necessary. They impose a degree of order that enables the human mind to cope with the otherwise overwhelming complexity of politics and war. However, they may also generate friction and rigidity. Standardized strategies can be valuable as a point of departure for tailored strategies or as elements of larger tailored strategies. However, when the entire process is run by routine, the results are predictable strategies by default that adversaries can easily anticipate and counter.

The Fait Accompli

One class of strategic-level actions is worth considering as a distinct category. These are strategies in which the political and military goals are identical and can be achieved quickly, simultaneously, and in one blow. Done properly, these actions appear to be isolated events that are not part of larger, continuous military operations. More than raids or harassment, these actions aim to present the enemy with an accomplished fact, or *fait accompli*—political/military achievement that simply cannot be undone. In 1981, the Israelis became extremely concerned about Iraq's nuclear weapons development program. They launched an isolated bombing raid that destroyed Iraq's Osirak nuclear facility. The Israelis had no further need to attack Iraqi targets, and Iraq had no military means of recovering the lost facility.

A coup d'état is usually designed as a fait accompli. The political and military objectives are the same thing: seizure of the existing government. Noncombatant evacuations are also normally executed as faits accomplis. In a noncombatant evacuation, one country lands its troops for the purpose of evacuating its citizens from a dangerous situation, as in a revolution or civil war. Once the evacuation has been accomplished, the cause for conflict between the state conducting the evacuation and those engaging in the hostilities that led to it has been removed.

The fait accompli is another potential strategic pitfall. It is immensely attractive to political leaders because it seems neat and clean—even "surgical." The danger is that many attempted faits accomplis end up as merely the opening gambit in what turns out to be a long-term conflict or commitment. This result was normally not intended or desired by those who initiated the confrontation. In 1983, the Argentines assumed that their swift seizure of the nearby Falkland Islands could not be reversed by far-off, postimperial Britain and that therefore Britain would make no effort to do so. They were wrong on both counts.

Limited and Unlimited Wars

Another common error is the attempt to characterize a war as either "limited" or "unlimited." Such characterizations can be seriously misleading. While we can generally classify the political and military objectives of any *individual* belligerent in a war as limited or unlimited, seldom can we accurately

98

characterize the conflict itself as limited or unlimited. To do so may leave us badly confused about the actual dynamics of a conflict.

If we examine the conflicting aims of the belligerents in the Vietnam War, we can see that this was never a limited war from the North Vietnamese perspective nor should South Vietnam have pursued only limited political objectives. North Vietnam's political goal was the elimination of the South Vietnamese government as a political entity and the complete unification of all Vietnam under northern rule. The North Vietnamese leadership saw victory in this struggle as a matter of survival. While the North Vietnamese military strategy against the United States was erosion, against South Vietnam it was annihilation. The South Vietnamese leadership was weak, enjoying little legitimacy with a population that had no hope of conquering the North. Its only goal was to survive. The American strategy against North Vietnam was one of erosion. However, the United States was never able to convince North Vietnam that peace on America's terms was preferable to continuing the war.

All wars can be considered limited in some aspects because they are generally constricted to a specific geographic area, to certain kinds of weapons and tactics, or to numbers of committed combatants. These distinctions are the factors at work in a particular conflict, not its fundamental strategic classification. Another common error is the assumption that limited wars are small wars and unlimited wars are big ones. This confuses the scale of a war with its military and political objectives. Large-scale wars can be quite limited in political and/or military objectives, while a relatively small conflict may have unlimited political and military objectives. The U.S. action against Panama in 1989 can be considered a very small-scale war, but both its political and military objectives were unlimited. Panama's capacity to resist was annihilated, its regime was deposed, and its leader was put on public trial and imprisoned. It is possible that had the United States pursued more limited objectives, the result might have been a war of attrition much more destructive to both sides.

The strategic pitfall in characterizing wars as limited or unlimited is that such a label may lead to adoption of an incorrect strategy. This is particularly true in the case of limited wars. There are always temptations to limit the military means employed, even when the political objectives demand a strategy of annihilation. Such inclinations stem from the psychological and moral burdens involved in the use of force, the desire to conserve resources, and often a tendency to underestimate the enemy or the overall problem. Strategists must correctly understand the character and the resource demands of a strategy before they choose it.

Paralysis and Recklessness

Competent strategic-level decisionmakers are aware of the high stakes of war and of the complex nature of the strategic environment. Successful decisions may lead to great gains, but failure can lead to fearful losses. Some personalities instinctively respond to this environment with a hold-the-line, take-no-chances mentality. Others display an irresistible bias for action.

Unless we understand the specific problems, dangers, and potential gains of a situation, the two approaches are equally dangerous. Paralysis is neither more nor less dangerous than blindly striking out in the face of either threat or opportunity. Unfortunately, the very process of attempting to ascertain the particulars can lead to "paralysis by analysis." Strategy makers almost always have to plan and act in the absence of complete information or without a full comprehension of the situation.

At the same time, strategists must guard against making hasty or ill-conceived decisions. The strategic realm differs from the tactical arena both in the pace at which events occur and the consequences of actions taken. Rarely does the strategic decisionmaker have to act instantaneously. The development of strategy demands a certain discipline to study and understand the dynamics of a situation and think through the implications of potential actions. While it is often possible to recover from a tactical error or a defeat, the consequences of a serious misstep at the strategic level can be catastrophic. Boldness and decisiveness, which are important characteristics of leadership at any level, must at the strategic level be tempered with an appropriate sense of balance and perspec- tive.

The strategist's responsibility is to balance opportunity against risk and to balance both against uncertainty. Despite the obstacles to focusing on specific strategic problems and to taking effective action, we must focus, and we must act. Success is clearly possible.

Conclusion

"War is a matter of vital importance to the State; the province of life or death; the road to survival or ruin. It is mandatory that it be thoroughly studied."[1]

—Sun Tzu

"As in a building, which, however fair and beautiful the superstructure, is radically marred and imperfect if the foundation be insecure—so, if the strategy be wrong, the skill of the general on the battlefield, the valor of the soldier, the brilliancy of victory, however otherwise decisive, fail of their effect."[2]

—A. T. Mahan

W e have explored the nature of politics, policy, and the political entities that wage wars. We have examined the most fundamental aspects of national and military strategy and have identified the basic questions we must answer when considering the use of military means to gain political goals. We have examined some basic types of military strategies and the ways in which those strategies relate to political objectives. We have also considered some of the problems in translating our understanding of these strategic fundamentals into practical military action. Now we must ask, *What does this mean for us as Marines?*

The modern strategic environment poses a significant challenge for the United States and its armed forces. The collapse of the Soviet Union has changed the existing strategic environment from one dominated by bipolar considerations to one that is in transition. Long-suppressed ethnic, religious, and even personal hatreds have spawned an increase in local and interstate violence. Terrorism, civil wars, and secessions threaten to fracture existing states and break down regional order. The strategist can no longer be guided by the Cold War's overarching strategic concept of containment. That said, strategic thinking must adjust to the evolving strategic environment.

The Department of Defense 1997 Joint Strategy Review concludes that the 21st century security environment will be characterized by chaos, crisis, and conflict. Global instability will continue to arise from the world's littorals, where well over half of the world's population resides. Thus, naval

105

expeditionary forces will remain one of the U.S.'s most reliable and flexible tools of global influence both for today and into tomorrow. The Marine Corps will be at the center of our national security and military strategies for addressing these challenges. Therefore, Marines must possess the strategic skills and understanding necessary to participate effectively in this environment.

As we noted at the beginning, the United States Marine Corps does not make national strategy, nor even the military strategy for fighting a particular war. However, individual Marines may well play a role in the making of strategy. Moreover, the Marine Corps is often intimately involved in the execution of strategy, and its effective execution requires an understanding of both the intent and the context behind the strategy. Strategic execution is not simply carrying out a fixed plan. Rather, it is a complex matter of both initiating action and effectively responding to events as they unfold. Without proper grounding in the strategic situation, the political and military objectives of the strategy, and the strategic concept, Marines will not be prepared to adapt to changing circum- stances.

The individual Marine must appreciate the complexities and difficulties of strategy. Few Marines will be in a position to fully grasp the larger strategic picture, especially while in the field executing a mission. Nonetheless, a fundamental understanding of the problems of strategy will help Marines to appreciate the importance of their role and their unit's role. It will help Marines to understand the significance of constraints like rules of engagement and to understand why policy guidance is sometimes unclear or often fluctuates. In the increasingly complex operations of the post-Cold War era, an awareness of the short distance between tactical action and its strategic impact may help individual Marines or Marine leaders to avoid actions that damage the United States' interests or image. This awareness should not impede action, but instead assist Marines in the evaluation of their situation and provide the basis for an intelligent response.

Marines will also serve on staffs or in commands where strategic decisions are made. They must be prepared to participate intelligently, tactfully, and energetically in the strategy-making process. They must be prepared to ask tough questions concerning both political and military objectives and to advise our political leaders on the capabilities and limitations in the use of the military instrument.

There is no shortcut to strategic wisdom. While some have predicted that the United States will be able to control the course of future conflicts through "information dominance" or a "system of systems," Marines continue to believe that people, not systems or machines, define success in war. Success in military action whether at the strategic, operational, or tactical level will continue to depend greatly upon the judgment, experience, and education of our Marines. The concepts of this publication cannot be mastered without serious and ongoing contemplation. Neither can they be turned into a strategic template to be laboriously worked through on every occasion. We

must think about these concepts, internalize them, and constantly seek to improve our understanding of the strategic environment. Such an understanding, based on a professional
approach to the complexities of war and politics, is the essence
of "fighting smart."

> [T]here is no substitute for the judgment and intuition of ex-
> perienced and properly educated commanders.

> Our goal is to equip every Marine with the thinking ability to
> win on the battlefields of the 21st century.[3]

The Study of Strategy

1. Unknown.

The Strategic Environment

1. Michael Howard, "The Use and Abuse of Military History," *Paramaters* (March 1981) p.14.

2. Sir Julian S. Corbett, *Some Principles of Maritime Strategy* (Annapolis, MD: Naval Institute Press, 1988) pp. 8–9.

3. See Carl von Clausewitz, "War As An Instrument of Policy," *On War*, trans. and ed. Michael Howard and Peter Paret (Princeton, NJ: Princeton University Press, 1976) pp. 605–610.

4. Geoffrey Blainey, *The Causes of War* (New York: The Free Press, 1973) p.114.

5. *National Geographic* (September 1994) p. 32.

6. Based on the 1972, 1976, 1977, 1981, 1986, 1990, 1994, and 1996 versions of the *Statistical Abstract of the United States* distributed by the U.S. Bureau of the Census (Washington, D.C.).

7. For the best overall introduction to complexity theory, see M. Mitchell Waldrop, *Complexity: The Emerging Science at the Edge of Order and Chaos* (New York: Simon & Schuster, 1992).

See also Alan Beyerchen, "Clausewitz, Nonlinearity, and the Unpredictability of War," *International Security* (Winter 1992/1993) pp. 59–92.

8.   Corbett, pp. 8–9.

9.   John M. Collins, *Grand Strategy: Principles and Practices* (Annapolis, MD: Naval Institute Press, 1973) p. 167.

10.   Ibid., p. 168.

11.   Charles Tilly, ed., *The Formation of National States in Western Europe* (Princeton, NJ: Princeton University Press, 1975) p. 42.

12.   Lawrence H. Keeley, *War Before Civilization*, "Table 6.1, Annual Warfare Death Rates" (New York: Oxford University Press, 1996) p. 195.

13.   *Compton's Interactive Encyclopedia*, version 2.01VW, "Africa" (1994).

14.   Blainey, pp. 109–114.

15.   George Liska, quoted in Michael Sheehan, *The Balance of Power: History and Theory* (London: Routledge, 1996) p. 2.

16.   Clausewitz, pp. 566–573. Do not confuse this political idea with Clausewitz's closely related concept of the "culminating point

of the offensive" which is primarily an operational and logistical concept.

17. Clausewitz, p. 89.

18. See Edward J. Villacres and Christopher Bassford, "Reclaiming the Clausewitzian Trinity," *Parameters* (Autumn 1995) pp. 9–19.

Strategy: Ends and Means

1. President John F. Kennedy's address at the U.S. Naval Academy Commencement, Annapolis, Maryland, June 7, 1961. Reprinted in Theodore C. Sorensen et al., *Let the Word Go Forth: The Speeches, Statements, and Writings of John F. Kennedy* (New York: Delacorte Press, 1988) p. 243.

2. **Military strategy**: "The art and science of employing the armed forces of a nation to secure the objectives of national policy by the application of force or the threat of force." (Joint Pub 1-02)

3. **National strategy**: "The art and science of developing and using the political, economic, and psychological powers of a nation, together with its armed forces, during peace and war, to secure national objectives." (Joint Pub 1-02)

4. Col Dennis M. Drew and Dr. Donald M. Snow, *Making Strategy: An Introduction to National Security Process and Problems* (Maxwell Air Force Base, AL: Air University Press, 1988) pp. 27–28.

111

5.   Collins, p. 3.

6.   Diplomatic, economic, military, and informational instruments make up the instruments of national power. Joint Pub 0-2, *Unified Action Armed Forces (UNAAF)*, 24 Feb 1995. In earlier joint doctrine publications, *instruments of national power* were referred to as *elements of national power*, and the *informational instrument* was called the *psychological instrument*. The February 1995 edition of Joint Pub 0-2 updated this terminology.

7.   In a true civil war, two sides are fighting for ultimate control of the same state or nation. The American Civil War was a war of secession; had it succeeded, there would have been two independent nations in place of the old United States. We call it a civil war because the secession failed and the Union remained intact.

8.   Discussions in this publication of American Cold War strategies are strongly influenced by the analysis of John Lewis Gaddis, *Strategies of Containment: A Critical Appraisal of Postwar American National Security Policy* (New York: Oxford University Press, 1982).

9.   In classical military theory, the traditional term is *strategy of annihilation*. See Hans Delbrück, *History of the Art of War Within the Framework of Political History*, trans. Walter J. Renfroe, Jr., especially vol. 4, chap. IV (Westport, CT: Greenwood Press, 1985).

10. Strategy of erosion is known as strategy of attrition in classical military theory. The concepts are the same. We use the term erosion to avoid confusion with the tactical concept of attrition warfare. See Hans Delbrück, vol. 4, chap. IV.

Strategic Opposites

1. Robert Debs Heinl, Jr., Col, USMC, Retired, *Dictionary of Military and Naval Quotations* (Annapolis, MD: United States Naval Institute, 1966) p. 311.

2. There is a long tradition of military theory involving asymmetrical strategies. It appears in Chinese military theory most prominently in Sun Tzu and in the works of Mao Zedong. A particularly clear discussion appears in Edward O'Dowd's and Arthur Waldron's, "Sun Tzu for Strategists," *Comparative Strategy*, vol.10 (1991) pp. 25–36. British military thinker B. H. Liddell Hart propounded asymmetry in his theory of the "indirect approach" most powerfully in his books, *The British Way in Warfare* (London: Faber & Faber, 1932), *The Ghost of Napoleon* (London: Faber & Faber, 1933), and *Strategy* (New York: Praeger, 1954). See also Sun Tzu, *The Art of War*, trans. Samuel B. Griffith (New York: Oxford University Press, 1971) especially the introduction written by Griffith.

3. John Foster Dulles, "The Evolution of Foreign Policy," *Department of State Bulletin* (Washington, D.C.: Department of State January 25, 1954).

The Making of Strategy

1.   John Terraine, *A Time For Courage: The Royal Air Force in the European War, 1939–45* as quoted in Colin S. Gray, *War, Peace, and Victory: Strategy and Statecraft for the Next Century* (New York: Simon and Schuster, 1990) p. 8.

2.   Used as a simple but effective model of the command and control process, the observation-orientation-decide-act (OODA) loop applies to any two-sided conflict. For a detailed description, see MCDP 6, *Command and Control* (October 1996) p. 63.

3.   *Critical vulnerability* is a Marine Corps doctrinal concept that appeared first in FMFM 1, *Warfighting* (March 1989) pp. 35–36. The term *center of gravity* found its way into our strategic vocabulary via Clausewitz's *On War*. Clausewitz used the term frequently and in a variety of meanings. See Clausewitz, pp. 595–597. For a full discussion of *center of gravity* and *critical vulnerability*, see MCDP 1, *Warfighting* (June 1997) pp. 45–47.

4.   R. Ernest Dupuy and Trevor N. Dupuy, *The Encyclopedia of Military History From 3500 B.C. to the Present* (New York: Harper Collins, 1993) p. 952. See also: Shelby Foote, *Fort Sumter to Perryville* (New York: Random House, 1986) pp. 110–114.

5.   **Strategic concept**: "The course of action accepted as the result of the estimate of the strategic situation. It is a statement of what is to be done in broad terms sufficiently flexible to permit its use in framing the military, diplomatic, economic, psychological and other measures which stem from it." (Joint Pub 1-02)

6.   James Turner Johnson, *Just War Tradition and the Restraint of War*, "A Moral and Historical Inquiry" (Princeton, NJ: Princeton University Press, 1981) pp. xxii–xxiii.

7.   A. T. Mahan, *The Influence of Sea Power Upon History, 1660-1783* (Boston: Little, Brown, and Company, 1942).

Conclusion

1.   Sun Tzu, p. 63.

2.   A. T. Mahan as quoted in Heinl, *Dictionary of Military and Naval Quotations*, p. 311.

3.   Commanding General, Marine Corps Combat Development Command, before combined hearings of the Procurement and Research and Development Subcommittees of the House National Security Committee, March 29, 1997. This testimony can also be found in "Information Superiority," *Marine Corps Gazette* (June 1997) pp. 59–60.

CPSIA information can be obtained at www.ICGtesting.com
Printed in the USA
BVOW02s2054290715

410890BV00002B/212/P